LEGG OVER
DORSET

RODNEY LEGG

HALSGROVE

First published in Great Britain in 2011

Copyright © Rodney Legg 2011

British Library Cataloguing-in-Publication Data
A CIP record for this title is available from the British Library

ISBN 978 0 85704 106 7

HALSGROVE
Halsgrove House,
Ryelands Business Park,
Bagley Road, Wellington, Somerset TA21 9PZ
Tel: 01823 653777   Fax: 01823 216796
email: sales@halsgrove.com

Part of the Halsgrove group of companies
Information on all Halsgrove titles is available at: www.halsgrove.com

Printed and bound in the UK by the MPG Books Group

Contents

To Di Hooley

Foreword

This book will hopefully be its own justification, if I have written it well enough, as it is narcissism which I am having the audacity to share. It has been my hospital job since being unexpectedly struck down by a series of bodily malfunctions. Here, to overdose on the alliteration, is an autobiographical summary of debriefs, deeds, desires, dialogue, digressions, discourse, despatches and dreams.

My cherished inspiration, admittedly well over-the-top, has been a quotation from *Guardian* feature writer Patrick Wright who dubbed me a 'one-man Dorset cultural institution'. Fanny Charles concurred in the *Blackmore Vale Magazine* by referring to 'Rodney Legg, arch-scourge (then and now) of politicians, governments, the military and the Establishment in general'.

The battle honour from my days as a proselytising journalist, as he handed over a bundle of deeds to my solicitor, Maurice Jensen, was that Jeremy Pope of Eldridge, Pope and Company called me 'a scurrilous ragmonger'. In another precious slanderous aside, author John Fowles observed that 'Rod could have been a perfect 1940s' spiv'. Publisher Peter Shaw told *The Observer* that 'Rodney's got an ego the size of a 20-ton truck'.

Such statements go to my head. They are, however, arguable or aspirational and will infuriate more people than they please. How Rodders got here may merit explanation. Current publisher Steven Pugsley suggested, though I hardly needed encouragement. His team at Halsgrove have already produced 39 of my books (yes, the word prolific applies). Julian Davidson came up with the title. I'll take them at their word before they change their minds.

−1−
A Feral Childhood

Lying in the pram, abandoned at the bottom of the garden, is my earliest memory. That was at 21 Easter Road in the Bournemouth outer suburb of Moordown, where I emerged in a home-birth on Friday 18 April 1947. My 43-year-old mother had struggled with me inside her through the longest permafrost in living memory, in a land crippled by austerity, debt, inflation, power-cuts, rationing, shortages and strikes. Mr Attlee's post-war Britain was being likened to a country under foreign occupation.

The pregnancy was unexpected. I was 'a mistake' as Aunt Effie used to point out. No one explained why they called me Rodney, though it was the name of a 33,900-ton battleship. *Nelson* and *Rodney* were the first British warships to mount 16-inch guns.

Mum parked my pram beside the compost heap because I was prone to cry a lot. Continuously, they said. I protested throughout on being baptised into the Church of England, in St Birinus Mission Church, across the road from home on 22 June 1947. There was a photograph of me bawling as a baby – lying in a cradle on the grass – beside a New Forest stream. 'Music at Linford', my father captioned it.

Ted Legg was a cobbler with a shoe-shop on Peters Hill in Winton. He was remarkably gentle and always doing practical things – such as putting new wheels on a woman's pushchair – for a succession of friends, relatives and strangers. Smells of the workshop imprinted upon me for life were freshly-cut leather with a heady mix of glue and solvents redolent of pear-drop flavour boiled sweets.

Paternal Dorset roots included a clutch of Hardys in Wareham and ageing Leggs across the county from Powerstock to Cranborne Chase. In the 1841 census my great-great-grandparents, Hester and James Legg, appear at Bockhampton on the next page to one-year-old Thomas Hardy. Arthur Legg – an 8th Army despatch rider known for his smuttiness as 'Dirty Uncle Arthur' – used to remind us at family gatherings that we belonged to Dorset rather than Hampshire:

> *'Be I Hampshire, be I buggery!*
> *I be up from Wareham.*
> *I know a girl with calico drawers*
> *and I be goin' to tear 'em.'*

Gladys Legg with sons Rodney and Barrie, at Cub Camp in Highcliffe, 1947

My mother was born Gladys Alexander at Primrose Cottage, Binfield, Berkshire. She came to Bournemouth in 1921 as favourite maid to Revd Lumley Green-Wilkinson when he moved from Ascot to St Peter's Vicarage on the East Cliff, facing the Royal Bath Hotel, having taken charge of the town's Mother Church. Both my father and mother were quiet and energetic workers rather than talkers. Not at all like me. On visits to the grandparents in Binfield I remember carrying around a stuffed jay, as swarms of wasps became drunk and listless on fermenting plums, and making friends with the pig in a sty at the bottom of the garden.

Ration coupons were still being handed over by my mother at the Co-Op in Malvern Road, Bournemouth. I was taught to give the dividend number (and also to know my address, as a toddler, 'so you can tell a policeman if you get lost'). I well remember my first punch. The person I hit was Revd Canon Percy Luker, vicar of St John the Baptist Church in Wimborne Road. That was a sharp jab to the paunch. I was four-years-old and he was playfully engaging with my brother Barrie (14) at Sea Scouts camp beside Buckler's Hard on the Beaulieu River. 'Don't you touch my brother', I told him.

I later perfected a throttle from behind coupled with balancing pressure to the middle of the spine. Instant submission. No one ever bullied me. I cut my own furrow as a practising loner and was always so different from Barrie. In the great Darwinian controversy of the nineteenth century, leading supporters were second sons, who tended to be opposed by first-born or only sons.

Childhood double fears for me were 'having your tonsils out' and 'your turn coming' when it came to the call-up for National Service. Tantrums succeeded in ensuring that I avoided the former. The latter fate was removed by abolition. Then I was grateful to Harold Wilson for vetoing British involvement in the Vietnam War because conscription could have been reinstated. Through the

Rodney at Binfield, Berkshire, in 1950

Beach boy Rodney Legg at
Studland in 1949

Rodney, Gladys, Barrie and Ted Legg at Keyhaven,
near Lymington, in 1953

Rodney with stuffed jay, at
Binfield, in 1951

Rodney Legg, with bell and rosette, at Charminster
Infants School on Coronation Day in 1953

The Legg family home at 21
Easter Road, Bournemouth

Rodney and Gladys Legg, with a wartime German
helicopter, at Farnborough Air Show in September
1953

Father Ted Legg was a cobbler at Peters Hill, Winton, Bournemouth

winter of 1956-57 I suffered repetitive nightmares featuring Soviet tanks that smashed their way into Budapest to end the Hungarian Uprising.

Brumas, named for the polar bear born in London Zoo, was my first golden hamster in 1953. For a while, like my friend Malcolm Noyes, I went into competition with Gerald Durrell who had just published *The Overloaded Ark* and set-up his own zoo in Ferndown, to opposition from bureaucrats and the locals. Soon my little menagerie went wild with minnows, lizards, newts, frogs and a huge common toad, plus countless hedgehogs – which successfully bred – and finally a fox cub, before settling down to contentment with a couple of cats.

Malcolm went the 'whole Durrell' with endangered French-bred mongoose lemurs from Madagascar. Philosophically, I think obsessive adoption of animals comes as compensation and reciprocation for an innate tendency towards animal cruelty that is inherent in all humans. It appears at its strongest in childhood. Those of us who over-react against it go to the other extreme, in a guilt-trip of well meaning intervention, to challenge what nature intended. Most are flawed from the start.

In my free time I was always in perpetual motion. It ran in the family as sunny Sundays were always outdoors, to the coast and countryside, for me to tick off ancient monuments and the parents to enjoy a picnic. The original car was an old Jowett with running boards, which Dad yearned to replace with an iconic modern Jowett Jaguar, but in the real world this turned into boring but reliable Standard Eight OEL 427.

The first time I watched television – a baby set in the corner of neighbour Mrs Sprague's living room – was for a cowboy series. It was shortly after the Queen's coronation but before Independent Television came to the screen. I missed that first night, on Thursday 22 September 1955, because at home we were loyal to the wireless. I know I was there as I can still visualise Grace Archer being engulfed by the stable fire in Ambridge. Next night, however, I did see it – and the sparkling toothpaste commercial for Gibbs SR – when Mum and I made our weekly visit for an evening with Aunt Effie Legg and Uncle Frank Watts. Television was love at first sight, from *Quatermass and the Pit* through to *Face to Face* with John Freeman and *That Was The Week That Was*. Eventually it turned to hate, in that for years I have been totally immunised, and would now top myself rather than endure national average exposure (3 hours 50 minutes per day). Exceptions could be made for Sergeant Bilko in the *Phil Silvers Show* and John Cleese in *Fawlty Towers*. I failed to find Charlie Chaplin, Eric Morecambe and Peter Sellers even remotely funny; nor anyone who amused brother Barrie.

Having long been 'statistically immeasurable' in not owning a television, I continue to be plagued by threatening letters from the licensing authority's Bristol headquarters, adamantly refusing to believe that someone in Britain does not have a set. I am therefore delighted to hear of fellow deniers, such as Mary Killen, in *The Times* on 20 March 1993. Her young brother-in-law, Pip Wood, likened television to a Chinese meal:

'Well, while you are watching it, you think you are watching something really interesting. Then afterwards you cannot remember a thing about it.'

In growing up, my strengths were in argument and logic and weaknesses impatience and poor co-ordination. That, coupled with being left-handed, did at least have the advantage of ensuring no one wanted me in their sports team. These days a diagnosis would range from attention deficit disorder to autism (most likely Asberger's if I had aspirational parents). Quite the reverse. My father despaired of me being able to do anything to earn an income, though I was happy enough doing three paper-rounds (morning, evenings and Sundays) and delivering milk on Saturday mornings.

'Penny for the Guy', between the Moderne and Ritz cinemas was a nice little annual earner for best friend Norman Chislett and myself. We also scoured the town in the summer holidays in the profitable cause of old-fashioned recycling. Glass bottles were collected from the beach to redeem their deposits. Paper and cardboard was piled high on the go-cart. Clothes and metal were a variation on the theme as we turned into juvenile rag and bone men. Conveniently, waste paper merchants Alexander and Son (known as Powell's) were in the middle of suburbia, in nearby Muscliffe Road. With Mum I had collected fir-cones and kindling wood on the town's former Poor Commons – now golf courses – but Norman and I tweaked the concept of free fuel by bringing home the occasional tar-soaked telegraph pole.

It was Mum who taught me to read, in fairy-cycle days at the onset of state

Rodney's Davy Crockett phase, during
Barrie Legg's Brylcreem period, in 1955

Barrie and Rodney Legg with Norman
Chislett (right) and bantams, in
Bournemouth, 1956

Rodney with aunt Dorothy Crocker (right)
at Beaconsfield model village,
Buckinghamshire, 1955

Barrie Legg with Rodney and goat at
London Zoo in 1956

education and the crowning of the Queen. The motivation, going fast forward
from comics, was Barrie's pile of gung-ho Biggles adventures. I still have a copy
of *Biggles, Pioneer Air Fighter* (ex-libris Nigel Gilbert from Crichel Road in
Winton). My hero from a classic was David Balfour in Robert Louis Stevenson's
Kidnapped though I was unaware at the time that this had been written in
Bournemouth. Added to these was each new war story as it appeared in
paperback. Plus cigarette and tea-card albums, I-Spy books, Rupert annuals and
the Observer series.

The impediment for me going on to write was left-handedness. When I was

Barrie Legg and Rodney, in Winton Secondary School tie, 1959

young it did not qualify one for membership of the master-race. Form teacher Miss Thomas would snatch the pen from that hand and push it into the helpless other. For centuries, writing with live ink, the method assumed you were right-handed, to drag a wet nib across the page in a hand that rested on virgin paper.

Doing this in reverse, I would push the pen into the grain of the paper – causing blots – and then smudge the results with my palm. To make things worse for Miss Thomas the content appalled her. Such as my project on the Second World War. Refusing to look at it, she said that war was brutality and violence, but I also reminded her of being in love. Total war, a decade gone, had taken Miss Thomas's sweetheart. Further cruelty for me was humiliation and ridicule for shambolic attempts at country dancing.

That torment at Summerbee Primary School ended with an awful 11-plus. Firstly, all my fish in the class aquarium were dead in the water under a cloud of graphite dust from mass pencil sharpening. Secondly, our class had never been confronted with a single IQ-type puzzle or question, whereas the 'chosen' next-door class had been doing them for weeks. As a result I went to Winton Secondary School for Boys.

I was required to attend Sunday School at the High Anglican parish church of St Francis of Assisi, Charminster, and was confirmed as a member of the Church of England. My questioning attitude agonised Father Julian Rudd. It infuriated an elderly spinster that I moved on the trot, behind the seats, replacing kneelers, Bibles and prayer books after services. 'Don't be so irreverent', she remonstrated. I admonished her, saying the fault lay with those who left the place strewn with debris, and asked:

'Why should God's work be done inefficiently?'

It left me ever-ready to put down self-proclaimed religious people. Under-age exposure to hymns and prayer gave me a lifelong appreciation for the finest words in the English language. That scriptural heritage still trips off the tongue at apposite moments, such as when I was reprimanded by a rector for cutting down some scrub, to open up a view he had not realised was there:

'Lift up mine eyes unto the hills.'

My mother shared my pragmatic view of religion. When the mission church and hall opposite our former home was sold by the Church of England, to the Lutherans, she voted with her feet and joined the German community. It appalled the vicar, Revd Reuben Henthorne, and those who still mentioned the war, which hardened her resolve. She became caretaker of the building. The congregation reciprocated by taking her on holiday to Hannover.

Throughout childhood, I saw all the popular movies at matinee showings, usually from a front of gallery corner seat at the Westover, including war films from *The Cruel Sea* to *The Longest Day*, Ealing comedies, the *St Trinian's* series and epic westerns like *Stagecoach* and *High Noon*. By the time I was teenager I had my own typewriter and, unusually for a male, could touch-type. Subsequent words can be blamed on teacher David Popham ('his English is more mine than his') who also happened to be a Dorset devotee. I was a constant disappointment to mathematician Victor Loosemore. 'Legg's Eleven' headmaster Stephen Lindley said to hilarity as my result was reported. Oddly, whilst algebra and logarithms remain a foreign country, I am fascinated by arithmetic and statistics.

Relations with teachers was not helped by having a letter published in the *Daily Express* denouncing the requirement that we should wear school caps as

Norman Chislett and Rodney Legg at play

13

Gladys and Rodney Legg at Stonehenge in 1960

Rodney habitually did his homework on the floor

'petty dictatorship'. I was already upsetting the Establishment. When I surprised everyone and came top of the class in the 1960 examinations, Lindley denied me the expected reward, because:

'... the boy West had done a better year's work, although he only came second in the examinations, and therefore the form prize was awarded to him.'

My cherished moment of revenge came when religious educationalist Robert Westerman invited a missionary friend from India to address the whole school. He primed five boys to ask simple questions at the end. Instead, I stood up, and interrogated the poor man on the forced integration of Nagaland. Westerman fumed but headmaster Lindley – visibly 'dead bored throughout' according to my contemporary notes – enjoyed the intervention.

A sense of injustice lasts longest when it starts young. I opted out at 16 with the General Certificate of Education for five O-levels (the same number as the Prince of Wales).

For ten years I grew up enjoying complete freedom and taking risks. It started with a go-cart, regularly down Homeside Road and into bushes beside West Way, with the inevitable scrapes and bruises. While attending junior school I cycled all over Bournemouth, Poole and Christchurch, then alone to Corfe Castle at age eleven, and on to Stonehenge as a teenager. Throw in free-style cliff climbing and walking up the Bourne Stream with Norman – through culverts and under the bridges – from Pier Approach to Coy Pond.

Add odd acts of delinquency and vandalism ranged from steaming through neighbours fences at night to starting a heath fire in high summer. At Shillingstone Station I shot out a window with an air pistol, from a steam train, to make my mark on the Somerset and Dorset Railway. Through it all I got off lightly, with no punishment or broken bones, and just a single scar. That was a tear to my right buttock from sliding into broken glass. I also avoided sexual abuse with the exception of being grabbed and kissed by a middle-aged man in a raincoat as I was entering the lift from the book department in Bright's store.

I was collecting all kinds of Dorsetiana – artefacts, books and ephemera connected with the county – and digging into Roman pottery kilns. By 1960 I was well into the process of visiting every prehistoric burial mound in Dorset – upwards of 2,000 – along with hill-forts and stone circles. The closest I came to being wiped-out was to suddenly turn my bicycle across the fastest stretch of the A354, virtually under the wheels of a driver I had not heard or seen, into a track on Gussage Down. Fortunately for me his reactions were instantaneous. That my guard dropped so low shows how intermittent and rare the traffic could be in post-war England.

Expeditions beyond normal cycling range started on the train to Dorchester and continued with an extended right-hand thumb to hitchhike into the hills. I found previously unrecorded mounds which were duly reported to field archaeologist Leslie Grinsell.

So ended a feral childhood. There could be no going back, my mother decided, as she followed St Paul's advice and gave my toys to younger cousins, a loss I shall never forget as long as there are auction records for a Hornby-OO train set headed by *Caerphilly Castle*. I can still remember the titles of a box of books that disappeared from the garage, particularly one withdrawn because of a libel case, and a blue-clothed tome on British constitutional law. My first job, for six months in 1963, was as a clerk at Atomic Energy Establishment on Winfrith Heath, followed by four years as a reporter for the *Basildon Standard* in Essex.

Fortunate enough to be rejected by the Bournemouth *Evening Echo*, and narrowly spared the task of collecting lists of mourners for the *Western Gazette*, I found myself 'dropped in at the deep end' as a 16-year-old on arrival in an under-staffed news-room at Pitsea. Nepotism got the job as big brother Barrie Legg – ten years older than me – played cricket with chief reporter Peter Lucas. Our old-school photographer, Bob Wall from Wickford, was soon joined by young-Turk Don McPhee, ex-Wilmslow and destined to become the *Guardian*'s outstanding cameraman for the next three decades. Peter Allen, on the next desk, graduated from Essex sports to Westminster politicians and is now with BBC Radio 5.

Basildon New Town sprawled towards us, with its diaspora of East Enders uprooted streets at a time, bringing a heady mix of arson, booze, crime, demolitions, murder, sex and suicide. There were weekly death-crashes at intersections along the Southend Arterial Road, attempts at sabotaging trains, and human interest stories of the kind we never read about at home. I watched a boy's body being lifted from a tidal weir where he had drowned, spoke to his friend, and phoned a 'Stop Press' paragraph to a London evening newspaper before anyone else knew. Unethical now – to release names before the family had been told – but I uncaringly floated on the adrenaline surge of constantly unfolding events. I still miss the excitement.

–2–
Last Empire Loyalist

The interlude between the end of austerity and the arrival of the Beatles happened to coincide with my teenage years and was marked nationally by a red mirage of political protest. In my case, perhaps because I came from Bournemouth, the colour was different. I identified with the reactionary true-blue backlash and joined the League of Empire Loyalists, an ultra-Conservative pressure group, which had been founded in 1954. I heard about it as a result of colourful stunts, aimed at embarrassing politicians, of the sort that newspapers report. They were by no means without risk to the participants, having led to violent backlashes such as that to which the conductor Sir Thomas Beecham alluded in *Frederick Delius*, his biography of the composer, in 1959:

> *'. . . a mighty howl of execration followed by the kind of treatment meted out to hecklers at our admirable present-day political party demonstrations.'*

My boyhood love for the British Empire became a political imperative. I was reading more about current affairs and politics at the age of 15 in 1962 than anyone else I met, almost entirely by proxy, in doorways across Moordown as I delivered morning, evening and Sunday newspapers (plus journals and magazines). On Saturdays I caught up with more esoteric material in the newspaper reading room upstairs in the Central Library at the Lansdowne. I found the address for the League in the classified advertisements at the back of the right-wing publication *Time and Tide* and sent the proceeds from a week's paper rounds, in postal orders for 12s 6d.

As a result of this and further small donations, bundles of leaflets started arriving from London, with headings like 'Keep Britain's Bomb' and 'Stop Coloured Immigration'. These I delivered around prosperous parts of Bournemouth, such as Queen's Park and Meyrick Park. I also started writing letters to newspapers, as far up country as the *Birmingham Post* and *Yorkshire Post*, and soon had a small network of sympathetic contacts and correspondents.

It became inevitable that I would be invited to visit the League's headquarters which was a basement office at the very heart of Empire. No. 11 Palace Chambers, Bridge Street, was in the block opposite Big Ben, in the triangle between Westminster tube station, the Red Lion tavern and Cannon Row police station. Its telephone number was TRA (for Trafalgar) 3881. Portcullis House, with the secretarial and research offices of Members of Parliament, stands on the site of Palace Chambers.

Our cluttered one-room base was run by Miss Avril Walters (early 20s – attractive, slim, vivacious and qualified as a lawyer, LL.B) and Austen Brooks (early 40s – burly, ginger-bearded and convincing enough in fancy dress, as a Greek Orthodox priest, to pass for Archbishop Makarios of Cyprus). Austen spiced his conversation with Gilbert and Sullivan moments and ended life as a sub-editor on the *Evening Echo* in Bournemouth where with wife Geraldine he could 'keep an eye on Rodney'. A Royal Navy lieutenant in a destroyer in the Mediterranean he recalled the signal from Admiral Sir Andrew Cunningham to 59-year-old Vice-Admiral Sir James Somerville KCB, Flag Office Force H at Gibraltar, on being appointed KBE on Trafalgar Day in 1941:

> *'Congratulations – twice a knight at your age.'*

As 'the last activist to join' the League of Empire Loyalists I was quoted by *Guardian* journalist Martin Walker in his book *The National Front*, published in 1977, with details of how its leader – Arthur Kenneth Chesterton who we knew as 'A.K.' – often paid our subsistence and travel expenses out of his own pocket:

> *'So many supporters were old that our membership declined with every post and every obituary column . . . Not only were we running out of money but the name was ceasing to be credible. People did know of the League's existence but that was no longer enough. The title was anachronistic. Political realities had made it a joke.'*

I travelled the country by train, where possible, or resorted to buses, hitchhiking, and using my feet. Once, arriving on the platform at Basingstoke as the last train for Bournemouth was a red light receding into the dark, I walked across the Hampshire Downs to Winchester, carrying a travelling bag and a 'portable' Remington typewriter. The night was memorable for one field with a stampede of horses around its edge and a huge snorting hedgehog in the middle. At dawn I was overtaken by the first trains of the day. This might sound an easy plod – just following the railway – but the line soon disappears into tunnels.

Before any event, activists would meet in the saloon bar of a discreet but findable public house, within reasonable walking distance of the venue concerned. From then on we were on our own, dispersed and mingling with genuine participants, until meeting up afterwards. Chesterton let us loose with three basic orders – 'get the League's name across, do not use any violence, and never interrupt anyone who is a guest to this country'.

The last instruction meant that though I could challenge or interrupt any British personage, including those from anywhere in the British Empire, I was never to abuse or criticise a visitor from elsewhere in the world. That applied irrespective of race or religion. The results could often verge on the farcical, in that I would hear out main speakers such as U Thant from the United Nations

Reporter Rodney Legg with his Remington portable

Most news was gathered by telephone

Rodney emerging from a priest's hole at Great Chalvedon Hall, Pitsea, photographed by Don McPhee in 1965

Rodney Legg in 1967

and then hector his hapless English chairman who would wonder what on earth he had said that was so wrong.

Before meeting back at the rendezvous for a drink and debriefing we made for a public call box to contact the media, usually via the country's two national news agencies, the Press Association and Exchange Telegraph.

My first outing was to the Somerset Hotel, Weymouth, and the Alexandra Gardens Theatre where we found two victims. They were the former Colonial Secretary, Iain Macleod, and his protégé Angus Maude, standing for the radicalised liberal wing of the Conservative Party in the South Dorset by-election. In effect, at a public meeting in Weymouth on 20 November 1962, we were supporting an independent anti-Common Market candidate, Sir Piers Debenham of the West End department store, via Briantspuddle, who was also in the rare position of receiving the support of the constituency's former Tory Member of Parliament, Viscount Hinchingbrooke. He had been forced to give up his seat in the House of Commons – causing this by-election – on succeeding his father as Earl of Sandwich. Hinchingbrooke used the law pushed through Parliament for the benefit of a reluctant 2nd Viscount Stansgate (MP for Bristol South-East, the Hon. Anthony Wedgwood Benn) to disclaim the peerage for his lifetime. Dorset's 'Hinch', reduced to plain Mr Victor Montagu, was treated as a traitor by former friends and never sat in the Commons again. He retired to Mapperton Manor in the hills above Beaminster.

My initial interruption was utterly formulaic as it articulated a slogan painted in yellow letters along the parapet of Pokesdown railway bridge in Bournemouth. It remained readable for another 20 years: 'Empire Loyalists say be British not Yankee puppets.'

'You are even bigger fools than you look', Macleod told us. 'We'd rather be fools than traitors', Austen Brooks retorted. It was in Chatham that he came out with the best heckle in recorded history. 'Why is it that I say the Royal Navy is vital for Britain?' Harold Wilson asked, with a rhetorical pause. 'Because you are in Chatham!' Brooks answered.

Our local MP, John Eden, suffered the indignity of being shouted down in his own constituency, on 14 December 1962. The blame for the barracking was attributed to Empire Loyalists (plural) who happened to be me (singular). This public meeting in St Peter's Hall, Bournemouth, was on the issue of joining the Common Market. Eden's mistake was to defy his audience. 'There will be no vote taken in the hall', he told us. 'Why not?' I asked and then answered for him, 'Because you'd lose it!'

'Keep the Bomb and fire the Canon . . .' My one and only attendance at an Aldermaston March ended in the firm hands of a black steward (who must have been somewhat aggressive as the unacceptable 'n' word slipped into my notes) and other assorted CND-ites on 15 April 1963. It was Easter Monday, in Hyde Park, and Avril Walters had just emptied an eight-pound bag of flour over the head of the chairman of the Campaign for Nuclear Disarmament, Canon John Collins of St Paul's Cathedral. He was dusted down to the strains of protest music and peace poetry.

I'm not at all sure what else happened on the way out, except that Avril lost her watch (though it was handed in by an honest pacifist) and I later walked back across Westminster Bridge from the Red Lion in Parliament Street, to board the 21.20 train from Waterloo. That night, not unusually, I went home on foot from Bournemouth Central Station (two miles, without the benefit of street lights which mostly went out before midnight) and was infatuated with Avril Walters. What it was, in those early hours of Tuesday with hedgehogs scurrying across empty roads, to think of being in love. I was two days away from my sixteenth birthday.

'Silence for the friend of Mau Mau', which seems to have became my catchphrase, was shouted first as Conservative Party chairman Iain Macleod stood to introduce by-election candidate Angus Maude to the voters of Stratford-upon-Avon on 7 August 1963. To us, Maude who had been rejected by Dorset voters (letting in Guy Barnett for Labour), was 'floating like froth on a tide of by-elections'. Austen Brooks completed his introduction: 'Silence for the rat returning to the sinking ship.'

As MP for Ealing South, Maude had taken a stand against Suez and rejected Conservative whip, to sit out his term as an independent in 1957. He was in the company of other principled younger Tories like Julian Amery, Harry Legge-Bourke and the aforementioned Hinchingbrooke. They held our respect but Maude had quit the rebellion and scuttled off to Australia. Scuttle and Suez were iconic words for Empire Loyalists because before my time we had presented a coal-scuttle to Prime Minister Anthony Eden in his own constituency at Warwick Castle. Missiles also featured, with denouncements of the abandoning of Blue Streak – and 'What happened to Blue Water and Blue Steel?' – in the wake of the American 'Skybolt betrayal'.

Randolph Churchill, Sir Winston's son, went into a rage and jumped to his feet a few feet behind us with a bellowing call to the chairman:

'I have travelled 150 miles to hear the Minister [Iain Macleod] speak at this meeting. Will your exercise your rights under the Public Meetings Act and tell these gentlemen that, if they keep on, they will have to be ejected.'

Randolph had come almost as far as me, from East Bergholt, in Suffolk. 'League members were in force in the town', *The Daily Telegraph* reported. 'Mr Macleod plodded on, in spite of almost constant interruptions. There were over 250 people in the audience.'

This time Maude, however, was back in Parliament, to be knighted in 1981 on retiring as Paymaster General, being created Baron Maude of Stratford-upon-Avon in 1983. Lady Barbara Maude remembered me from Weymouth and Stratford, when we found ourselves dining on adjacent tables at Holbrook House Hotel, Somerset. Recognition, on seeing my face, triggered a look of utter horror.

Back in 1963 we were playing the game of identifying the pseudonyms of characters named by Lunchtime O'Booze in *Private Eye*. Mr Silas Jones ('a West Indian immigrant of no fixed abode') was John Edgecombe. Miss Gaye

Funloving ('a 21-year-old model') was Christine Keeler. Dr Spook ('with more than half the Cabinet on his list of patients') was the osteopath Stephen Ward. Lord Blank (from a much-partying 'Berkshire estate') was Viscount Bill Astor at Cliveden. Mr Vladimir Bolokhov ('the well-known Soviet spy') was Eugene Ivanov. Mr James Montesi ('a well-known Cabinet Minister') was the Secretary of State for War, Jack Profumo. Emperor Macmilian ('the alleged Prime Minister') was Harold Macmillan whose grip on power waned as the scandal unfolded. The Conservative Party Conference in Blackpool that October was set to take stock on the winds of change that were blowing from Cape Town to Clivedon, as a ditty spread through the Westminster village:

'To lie in the nude is very, very rude, but to lie in the House is obscene.'

It was the great year of satire from *That Was The Week That Was*, on television, to performances on stage. On the evening of Wednesday 2 October 1963 I had a one guinea seat in the stalls at the Prince Charles Theatre, Leicester Place, in order to hear the 'Behan Bein' Behan' show. 'Salty, topical, irreverent', promised the *Scottish Daily Express*. There were four others with me to stop drunken Irish republican wit Dominic Behan in his tracks. This proved remarkably easy thanks to first-rate theatre acoustics. 'Keep the Royal family out of it' was the point we made.

Somewhat surprisingly we drew ripples of applause from the audience. The cause for objection was that a foreigner should not insult our monarchy in our country. Dominic – the brother of playwright Brendan Behan – hoped we might return the following night. 'My friends will be able to cope with them', he said. 'Most of my friends are ex-IRA . . .'

By then our attention was turning north for the principal event of the Empire Loyalist year. Forged tickets were being prepared. They should be passable at a glance, we were told, but not good enough for close scrutiny. By now I was adept at looking innocent, merging with the crowd, and slipping in between the coat-tails of others. Travelling separately, we were heading for the 'Mass Meeting' of the National Union of Conservative and Unionist Associations in the Empress Ballroom of the Winter Gardens at Blackpool. This was particularly important because Harold Macmillan was in the process of resigning as Prime Minister and there were three contenders for the succession. The Home Secretary, R. A. 'Rab' Butler, was the clear favourite.

The *Birmingham Evening Post* of 12 October 1963 reported on its front page:

'As in recent years, ever since Empire Loyalists had made a practice of interrupting Mr Macmillan when he had delivered the winding-up speech, elaborate precautions were taken against gatecrashers. Even so, before a word had been spoken, a raucous interruption, believed to be from an intruding Empire Loyalist came from a balcony at the back: "End this Government!" Twelve ushers marched an 18-years-old member of the League of Empire Loyalists from the ballroom as Mr Butler started to speak. Rodney Legg, of

Bournemouth, had interrupted several times.'

In fact I was only 16, but claiming an extra couple of years made it less likely that I would be taken into care or custody. My eventual exit took some time, as it unfolded in slow motion, and I began on Lord Home who was chairing the conference. 'You are scrapping the Royal Navy', I started. 'Why even discuss mixed-manned fleets? Keep the British forces in British hands. Empire Loyalists say no cosmopolitan fleet for Europe.' From naval matters I progressed to 'Empire Loyalists denounce the betrayal of Kenya to Mau Mau terrorists'. Home let me speak, and remain, until he had introduced Mr Butler.

'Silence for the friend of Mau Mau', I bellowed, drowning-out the opening of Butler's keynote speech. There was uproar. Then Lord Home rose – causing Butler to sit down – and ordered 'my young friend' to leave. I was already walking out at the time, between being grabbed and kicked, and raised my hand to wave at the television cameras. The stumbling performance of Rab Butler during and after this hiatus made him the Prime Minister we never had. That, in hindsight, was the conclusion Jonathan Friedland gave us in an edition of *The Long View* on BBC Radio 4 in 2005.

I targeted Butler particularly vigorously because he was the main speaker, a point not missed on Peregrine Worsthorne, in his front page report for *The Sunday Telegraph* on 13 October 1963. He sensed that the 4,000-strong audience would have preferred the 14th Earl of Home – the Foreign Secretary, who was chairing the meeting – to be addressing them:

'Nor did the chairman himself do much to help by allowing extremist hecklers an unprecedented freedom to interrupt Mr Butler, who was repeatedly forced to sit down while Lord Home called for quiet. No doubt his Lordship established himself as a delightfully tolerant man, with a nice regard for freedom of speech. But such unusual tolerance did not help poor Mr Butler, who might legitimately have expected greater protection from the chairman on such a delicate and difficult day.'

The other loser in the leadership struggle was Lord Hailsham who was in the process of becoming Mr Quintin Hogg, by disclaimed his peerage in order to contest a by-election. 'In the Conservative Party, leadership is a collective function', he said, in the hope of convincing himself that it might be true. The Tory Party had become more Ringo than Jingo as *Land of Hope and Glory* was dropped for *Getting to Know You* and *I'm in Love with a Wonderful Guy* when Sir Alec Douglas-Home addressed a rally in Newcastle.

Getting on television brought its backlash. There was an internal protest from St Helens, near Blackpool, where a Mr T. Franklin wrote to complain of 'the "whirling dervish" type of disturbance and the unintelligent type of heckling . . . for its own sake'. He also said that our leaflets should only be handed to 'clergymen and schoolmasters'. All other attempts at influencing hearts and minds were a waste of effort.

Avril Walters and I followed the victor – who reinvented himself as Sir Alec Douglas-Home – to Kinross in Perthshire for his Scottish by-election battle. We barracked his principal public meeting, to a capacity crowd of 600 in Aberfeldy, on 1 November 1963. 'Shouts halt Sir Alec's speech', a very drunk George Gale reported, on the front page of the following morning's *Daily Express*.

Apart from the ten minutes it took to phone through his copy, he was with us drinking at the hotel bar, through to 2 am. He spoke in the same clipped but descriptive way that he wrote, coloured with expletives, and was damning on the way the Security Service framed Stephen Ward as the scapegoat to distract public attention from those responsible for the Profumo scandal. Avril traded Westminster gossip about politicians Bob Boothby and Tom Driberg. *Great Parliamentary Scandals*, by Matthew Parris, shows that the former's alleged proclivities made news a few months later. Matthew also relays the story of Driberg providing oral sex to Nye Bevan in the Labour leader's office at the House of Commons. He writes as if he hopes it was true. 'Looking, brooding, disputing' were the recreations Gale listed in *Who's Who*. He was the original for *Private Eye*'s Lunchtime O'Booze. I see from his report that I introduced a topical theme to the Aberfeldy meeting, as chairman Major Neil Ramsay told us that Sir Alec was 'on his way to being returned':

'Send him back to the House of Lords!'

On the way home, breaking the journey in London to walk into Trafalgar Square with Peter Bleach, I carried a wide canvas banner as part of an march by the Anti-Apartheid Movement. We then succeeded in raising it outside South Africa House and had it prominently displayed, on the steps of the National Gallery, facing the speakers on the plinth of Nelson's Column. As the crowd spotted its dubious wording, the mood of fellow marchers turned ugly, and police intervened to remove us from the scene. The offending banner recalled an inglorious moment in the liberation struggle:

'Remember Cato Manor where the police were hacked to pieces.'

On 2 December 1963 I made my contribution to the main meeting in the Marylebone by-election by asking Quintin Hogg if he had read the Mau Mau oaths and details of their administration ceremonies (with blood, goats and much worse): 'Do you realise you have betrayed the white settlers of Kenya Colony to the convicted manager of Mau Mau?' Hogg was still talking about the disruption at his press conference the following day.

I was back in London on 12 December 1963, battling the same theme, as 3,000 guests filed into the Commonwealth Institute in Kensington to celebrate Kenyan independence. To quote from my notebook:

'After an unsuccessful attempt I gate-crashed. However I was too late and missed the speakers. Shouted (after having a couple of gins on the Kenyan Government) from the top floor – "Empire Loyalists denounce the betrayed

of the white settlers to Mau Mau. Kenya is the biggest betrayal in British history".'

I then released a shower of Mau Mau oath leaflets – documenting actual ceremonies – which had been printed with a warning: 'Do not let this fall into the hands of children or adolescents.' After the induction with bestiality and excrement came an instruction 'to kill no matter who is to be the victim, even one's father and brother' and then 'cut off heads, extract the eyeballs and drink the liquid from them', presented in alarmingly well-written English which does tend to diminish the virtues of education.

Sitting in the main hall of the Friends' Meeting House, Euston, on 15 February 1964 I looked the part as a Young Conservative. It was their annual rally, addressed by Prime Minister Sir Alec Douglas-Home, who told us that his Government had acted to stop 'chaos and strife' in Cyprus. 'This Government created chaos by handing Cyprus to the arch-terrorist Makarios', I shouted. 'Empire Loyalists were right and you were wrong . . .' With that, mid-sentence, a hand from behind covered my mouth and dragged me backwards.

'Now we shall never know what he was going to say,' the Prime Minister said as I was ushered out, though I did manage a final cry to 'Stand by the white man in Rhodesia'. From the corridor outside I was dragged into a side room, thrown on to the floor, interrogated about how I had slipped in, and had my pockets searched by a gaggle of more than a dozen stewards. They held me for more than 15 minutes in a state of increasing agitation.

The Sunday Telegraph had caught the moment of my capture in the hall with a front-page photograph of that hand across my mouth, though the accompanying report down-played what followed: 'It was easy-going stuff, and even the young Empire Loyalist was hustled out with almost decent good humour.'

More constructively, allowing me to articulate the cause, Malcolm Muggeridge gave seven of us – young Loyalists aged between 16 and 23 – half an hour to ourselves in the *Let Me Speak* slot on the new BBC2 network. I found myself in my element responding to ascorbic scepticism. Taking on Saint Mug or Smuggeridge was one convert combating another. I crossed London to Shepherd's Bush on a No. 11 Routemaster (the one that never dared to run over Mrs Thatcher) and since then have never willingly travelled by bus. The programme was broadcast on 15 August 1964.

I took on Nigel Fisher during the general election campaign of September 1964, when he spoke at Enfield West as the outgoing Parliamentary under-secretary of State for Commonwealth Relations and the Colonies. He talked about the V-bombers of our independent nuclear deterrent. 'What are you going to replace then with?' I asked. 'The American Polaris', he answered. 'That's not British, nor independent!' I screamed.

On 24 November 1964 I barracked veteran socialist Fenner Brockway as he addressed a meeting in St Pancras Town Hall. 'Empire Loyalists denounce the Movement for Colonial Freedom as a Communist front . . .' I was bellowing as my speech was halted by a flailing fist. Ironically, campaigning on environmental

SUNDAY TELEGRAPH

No. 159 · February 16, 1964 · Price 5d.

A firm hand stops Home's heckler

*Rodney Legg making
front page news
(foreground) on
16 February 1964*

issues a decade later I wined and dined Lord Brockway, was described as his 'protégé', and took him trespassing on a fact-finding mission across the Lulworth tank gunnery ranges in the Isle of Purbeck.

Back at home, on 29 November 1964, I was able to arrange a welcome for our former internationalist MP, Nigel Nicolson – rejected by Bournemouth East and Christchurch Conservative and Unionist Association in February 1959 – on his first public return to the constituency. He was in the town to deliver a talk to the local branch of the United Nations Association. His earlier links with Bournemouth had been undermined by an Empire Loyalist vendetta that started when he joined the Suez rebels. The son of Sir Harold Nicolson and Vita Sackville-West, who formed the intellectual half of publishers Weidenfeld and Nicolson, was the official historian of the Grenadier Guards. What Nicolson himself now described – with an uncomfortable smile – as 'my most persistent fan-club' were present in every row of the small hall.

He gave us the floor to make our points about United Nations atrocities in Katanga, its denouncements of Britain, and inaction from Hungary to Tibet. I asked why the United Nations had helped the spread of Communism by allowing Nasser's Egypt to colonise the Yemen. No attempt had been made to investigate poison bomb attacks on unarmed Yemeni royalist civilians. As light relief, Nicolson provided an anecdote on the Profumo affair:

'I would like to give you some idea of the character of the new Secretary General of the United Nations Organisation. U Thant invited me to his room

25

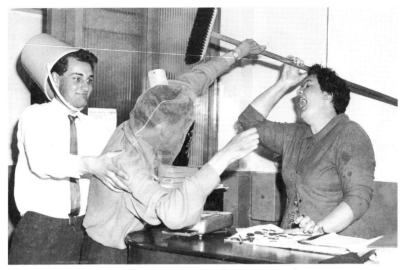

Playing at work – Don McPhee, Rodney Legg and Pam Lucas in the Basildon Standard *office, photographed by Bob Wall in 1966*

at the UN at the time of the Stephen Ward case. When I went in he was sitting at his desk, surrounded by newspapers from all over the world, in every part of which major and minor crises were raging. He looked up at me, as calm and imperturbable as ever, and said: "Good morning, Mr Nicolson. Tell me, Mr Nicolson . . . Is she a very pretty girl?"

Nigel Nicolson had joked at a previous meeting that one of his duties as chairman was to 'look under the table to see if Empire Loyalists have crept in'. In that case, also, they indeed had, which made for an amusing column at his expense in *The Times*.

The next by-election, in January 1965, was at Leyton where Labour's Patrick Gordon Walker – thrown out by an anti-immigrant vote from Smethwick in the October general election – failed again to return to Parliament. The Conservative victor and his voters were called 'lepers' by Prime Minister Harold Wilson who was determined to bring back Gordon Walker and had appointed him Foreign Secretary. Our part in his demise was to disrupt his main election meeting where 400 had crowded into the hall. Reactive heckling included my answer to his claim that Britain still held a 'counting role' on the world stage. 'Keep the TSR2 then!' was a protest at the scrapping of what the RAF regarded as the best British fighter since the Spitfire. 'There's no oppressed minority in Ghana . . .' he was telling us in a sentence which I completed '. . . because they're all in prison.'

'Are Leytonians lepers too?' the League asked in a telegram to Harold Wilson, reported by the *Daily Express* after Gordon Walker's defeat.

'So raise the scarlet standard high:
Beneath its shade we'll live or die.
Though cowards flinch and traitors sneer
We'll keep the Red Flag flying here.'

As Harold Wilson and the delegates rose to sing their revolutionary song to close the Labour Party Conference in Blackpool on 1 October 1965 I jumped up in a balcony of the Empress Ballroom in the Winter Gardens and produced a Union Flag. It had been rolled up and hidden in a poacher's pocket which my mother had sewn into my conspicuously non-Gannex mackintosh. 'Keep Britain free', I yelled. 'Empire Loyalists say this is the flag which stands for British loyalty – not the red flag of Communist tyranny.'

Later that month I repeated the trick, on Monday 25 October 1965, in Church House at Westminster. The Foreign Secretary, Michael Stewart, was there to address an international meeting. As he stood to speak I leapt forward and draped a Union Flag over the insipid blue rag of the United Nations Organization:

'Empire Loyalists say this is the flag which should command British loyalty, not the pale blue and white rag of the UN. The United Nations is the enemy of Rhodesia and of Britain. Empire Loyalists support friends, not our enemies.'

As I was being hustled out by stewards, the call was taken up by three other Loyalists – Peter Bleach, Rosine de Bounevialle and Avril Walters – with placards proclaiming that 'One man one vote equals one-party tyranny in Africa'. Another half dozen carried on with verbal protests after they had been removed.

There was a Union Flag draped across the rostrum for the League's twelfth annual meeting, held in the Lancaster Room of Caxton Hall, Westminster, on 30 October 1965. There were about 50 of us that Saturday, led by the committed core of Colonel Blimps (who ensured that the flag was displayed the correct way up) and even more war widows, though it was given to me as the new generation to propose the first of four resolutions:

'That this annual general meeting of the League of Empire Loyalists wishes to alert members and supporters of Her Majesty's Opposition to the fact that Great Britain's entry into the European Common Market is being introduced insidiously as a part of the Conservative Party's official policy, and reminds them that abandonment of sovereignty to the European Economic Community would be an act of treason.'

There was something of a mutual admiration society about the proceedings. For me, in presenting her report on the year's activities, Leslie Greene singled out the Blackpool performance:

'You will most of you have read of the most effective demonstration by Rodney Legg – a young man whose readiness to carry the war into the enemy's camp

27

never diminishes – at the Labour Party's conference . . . Rodney Legg – who is rapidly qualifying for the title of the League's Flag Lieutenant.'

The oddest thing about all this showing of the flag – only to have it confiscated – was that replacements were virtually unobtainable in London at that time. Having bought the biggest that were left at the Scout Shop in Buckingham Gate, much to the surprise of staff, we were told they did not know if anyone made them any more.

Edward Heath became the leader of the Conservative Party, in Opposition, in 1965. Family man Reggie Maudling had squared up ineffectually to the piano-fugue playing bachelor whose first supporting duo comprised Humphrey Berkeley and Roger Gresham-Cooke. I caught up with Heath at a Brighton rally though I am unsure of the date as I have lost the relevant cuttings and notes. By this time security was being tightened and gatecrashing was becoming increasingly difficult, towards the point of virtual impossibility, even before internment without trial across the water which brought the backlash of Irish insurrection to the mainland in general and its politicians in particular.

Getting of the street and into the foyer was relatively easy, merging with a cluster of Tory ladies, but then there were multiple barrier checks. I went leftward and hid behind columns and pillars, moving inwards and upwards into the building by stages as speeches began and controls were relaxed. On the way up the stairs I found a side door. Inside, huddled in the dark beside mops and brushes, beneath electrical switch-gear, I strained to listen to the peaks and troughs of words that were being carried along central heating pipes like a primitive form of home-made radio.

Having realised that it must be Edward Heath who was speaking I left my refuge and walked with as much confidence as I could muster, passing a single steward, through doors into the upper balcony. Fearing that Heath might be about to end at any moment, overwhelming me in a standing ovation, I started shouting almost immediately. The words were about Rhodesia – I think – and comprised a single sentence before I was swept off my feet by a rush of officials. As I was propelled though the swing doors they crashed back on either side with an enormous thud in authentic stereo. 'I hope that was his head', a lady remarked.

It was the turn of the Liberal Party when they held their annual rally in Westminster, at Central Hall on the Monday, 1 November 1965. My contribution this time was to interrupt their leader, Jo Grimond, as he endorsed Archbishop Ramsey's 'right' and 'wise' condemnation of Ian Smith's unilateral declaration of independence in Southern Rhodesia. 'Unlike you, they remain loyal to the Queen!' I told him. 'You want to turn Rhodesia into a second Congo.' We had mustered a team of ten and were almost relieved to be manhandled or otherwise thrown out so that we could adjourn to St Stephen's Tavern. There, contrasting with Liberal tedium, a political journalist entertained us with a story about Lord Boothby and a 16-year-old rent boy enjoying what in the House was known as a Tom Driberg moment.

The next meeting in Westminster was at Church House, where the Lord Chancellor, Lord Gardiner, sat on the platform with the Archbishop of

Canterbury, Lord Ramsey for a 'Human Rights Day' ceremony organised by Amnesty International. I opened the proceedings with a walk-out:

'My Lord Chancellor, while your Government is waging economic warfare on our kinsmen in Rhodesia these proceedings are farcical.'

In Whitehall, where the Armistice Day wreath from the Rhodesian Government was said to have been 'left in an attic at the Home Office' we made up for its absence with a larger substitute, which remained in place throughout the Remembrance Sunday ceremony and had its words jotted down by Fleet Street reporters:

'In honourable memory of our thousands of Rhodesian kinsmen who fought and died in two world wars to keep the Union Jack flying in Rhodesia, where it still flies.'

'Ground nuts' – a shout which could only have come from Austen Brooks – was a blast from the past recorded by the *Daily Telegraph*, as the Prime Minister addressed a mid-term election meeting in Chiswick Town Hall on 17 March 1966. The scheme, which was both a scandal and a shambles, was intended to produce peanuts as the principal colonial cash-crop for post-war East Africa. Fraud and incompetence included the delivery of miscellaneous tank parts to Dar-es-salam and Mombassa that had been crated-up as 'agricultural machinery'.

For my contribution from the past there was a 'Communist stooge' reminder to Wilson that he went to Moscow on a mission for Clement Attlee. More relevant was the belief of Empire Loyalists that Ian Smith in Rhodesia was a better exemplar of British values than Edward Heath in England. Wilson, his mental footwork as agile as that of Casius Clay, seized on this and retorted:

'Never did I think to see the day when the Conservative Party, from their aristocratic leaders to their equally intelligent stooges, would want to put the mantle of respectability around rebels against the Crown whom they are now supporting.'

In Dorset I discussed politics with a single close confidant. Ernest Hardy, from the Old Rectory in Godmanstone, in a second-hand bookshop at Church Street, Dorchester. An Austrian Jew, he had shown me his Auschwitz number, branded in blue on his wrist. Ernest took his surname after arriving in Dorset after the war and asking what was the 'best known name in the district'. He did not even know of the existence of the internationally famous novelist whose first editions he was now selling. 'If I had, I would have chosen yours instead', he said, after yet another customer had grilled him on his precise relationship to Dorchester's great man. Both of us brought baggage and were committed cynics.

My last public flag-waving took place at the Labour Party Conference in Brighton on 4 October 1966. Standing among journalists, I pulled out a Union Flag from under my coat, as Prime Minister Harold Wilson began his keynote speech. 'Empire Loyalists say stop waging economic warfare against Rhodesia', I shouted. 'This flag still flies over Salisbury, not the Red Flag of your conference.'

Francis Flavius reported in *Tribune*, on 7 October 1966:

'When Mr Wilson stood up to speak on Tuesday, a lone Empire Loyalist jumped up in the press seats and attempted to unfurl a Union Jack. Immediately two plain clothes police (or security men) sitting, by convenient coincidence, in the same row, leapt on the young man and hauled him out with utmost roughness . . . It was the sort of incident which leaves an unpleasant taste in the mouth. Does every eccentric interrupter of the Prime Minister have to be mauled in this brutal fashion.'

Alan Walters, who went on to be Mrs Thatcher's economic guru, concurred in the same day's *Spectator* under the loaded headline 'Death of a Conference':

'The man sitting at the end of the row reserved for newspapermen had large shoes and a card marked "Press" thrust rather too ostentatiously into his breast pocket. I did not recognise him as a colleague; nor did he carry a notebook. A few minutes earlier in the proceedings, at the beginning of the Prime Minister's speech, he, together with two other ostensible pressman, had fallen upon an Empire Loyalist demonstrator with what was in the circumstances an uncalled-for display of zeal, and had handed him over to the Labour Party stewards.

'It occurred to me to approach this new ornament of the profession and say: "You are Lobby Lud of the plain clothes branch and I demand my prize." I did not, however, take this course. In view of the jumpy state of the authorities – a harmless but bearded television man was told "We don't want any trouble here" – it was impossible to predicate the exact consequences of such a move. And, conscious as ever of my duty towards my readers, I was not particularly anxious to suffer the same fate as the Empire Loyalist.'

As with white Rhodesia, the League's fortunes were flagging. Membership had slumped from 3,000 in 1958 – still buoyant from 'the Suez factor' – to only 337 paid-up supporters when I last up-dated the record cards on a day-trip to our basement office. Something had to be done. On 8 October 1966, at the thirteenth and final annual meeting of the League of Empire Loyalists in the Kingsway Hall, London, I was the reporter for the purpose of taking down comments regarding a proposed merger with the British National Party.

The purpose was to form a National Front. League members, it was reluctantly agreed, were often regarded 'as old fashioned Kiplingesque relics of Victorian days' though the counter argument was that we were 'the most modern of movements' when it came to activities and demonstrations. My involvement survived the early days of the National Front. Andrew Fountaine, Norfolk landowner and British National Party president, introduced the League contingent at the inaugural meeting:

'They have done staggering things. With their five men and a boy they have made world headlines.'

Where and why we parted company was at a directorate meeting in London in May 1968, where I was given an unacceptable ultimatum. I detailed this for Martin Walker when he researched his book on right-wing politics. It was triggered by a vote to allow membership of the National Front to Greater Britain Movement leader and convicted self-styled Nazi para-military John Tyndall. Resistance was led by Andrew Fountaine but in the event there was only one other rebel apart from me:

> *'Chesterton was newly returned from South Africa and had decided to admit John Tyndall to respectability. It was the one thing I was prepared to make a stand on. A.K. came into the room at the end of the meeting. He had given an ultimatum and wanted our reaction. We had either to submit or get out. There was no compromise offered. His leadership was in question and a personality clash developed between A.K. and Fountaine. Andrew refused to back down and A.K. was equally stubborn in his determination to have a confrontation. He stood at the door, wearing a dirty raincoat, and demanded we approved his actions. Andrew walked out and Gerald Kemp and I went with him.'*

Extremist inmates had taken over the asylum with predictably unstable behaviour that soon began to appal Chesterton. He had always struck me as charismatic, handsome and suave. Even as he controlled the course of that meeting from the corridor he maintained something of that, if visibly dented by a sartorial lapse, though that may have been down to the cold weather. From now on, like Frankenstein, he could only despair at the monster he had created.

The National Front applied itself in establishing a reputation for general brawling, racial taunts and mindless chanting. Such gutter tactics were reciprocated in kind. Arrive at a meeting in a car and you could expect to return to slashed tyres. Those who stuck to the almost-moderate Chesterton line were dubbed 'the Sycophants'. They even attempted an 'Operation Shake-Up' but this turned into a counter-coup which saw the leader ousted whilst on his annual sojourn to Cape Town in the winter of 1970. Chesterton had only the past before him, as my politics reversed leftward, to win the cherished epithet 'as pink as poached salmon' from Cranborne Chase grandee Michael Pitt-Rivers.

In the general election of 1974, which saw the return of Harold Wilson as Prime Minister, I cast my customary spoilt vote in Milborne Port, Somerset. Such votes always receive attention as they are shown by the returning officer to each of the candidates. This was to be my last direct participation in the democratic process, having realised how easily traceable such token protests were, and their sensitivity now that Britain's colonial wars had been repatriated to haunt the north of Ireland. My contribution drew odd looks, due to the fact it took a minute for me to write it out in the booth, and was on behalf of a 44-year-old peace campaigner:

> *'Free all British political prisoners. Release Pat Arrowsmith!'*

-3-
The Fight for Tyneham

The day job of reporting in Essex was followed by a stint in London, as a production editor for Michael Heseltine's Haymarket Press, on the titles *Hi-fi Sound* and *Gardener's Chronicle*. Meanwhile, teenage political aspirations became fused with a stronger obsession, and subsumed into a fight to preserve the Dorset countryside. So many treasured memories were being desecrated by ploughing and development, that it was becoming as painful to love places as people. The Sixties had progress as its maxim. It was time for a backlash.

In Dorset this became epitomised by the cause célèbre that prompted the Ministry of Defence into turning the Lulworth Ranges into an exemplar of military ecology incorporating public access. My initial return to Dorset, with first partner Colin Graham from Southend-on-Sea, was to a semi-derelict Coneygar Farmhouse beside the bridleway from Shillingstone to Hammoon. Living conditions were not helped by landlord Alec Cross developing a habit of turning off our water, at the stop-cock in his farmyard, at random times both day and night.

The first shot in the Tyneham campaign was an article for *The Countryman* which editor John Cripps turned into an opinion piece. It grew into a 'Surrender Purbeck' feature, accepted for publication and set in type, for the *Dorset Year Book* in the winter of 1967-68. The editor, Nat Byles, spiked it at the last moment, fearful of establishment reaction. That provoked me into producing an independent organ to publish it, by founding my own *Dorset – the county magazine* which continues to this day, produced in Wareham by John Newth, though now with the title *Dorset Life*.

In it I called for the formation of a Tyneham Action Group. Monica Hutchings from Church Knowle, author of doctor-nurse romances and topographical books, supported the campaign with an evocative slide-show which toured the Women's Institute circuit. Canon Edward Brooks, vicar of Fordington, provided the Moule Institute in Dorchester for a public meeting on 18 May 1968.

The *Daily Telegraph* called me 'the driving force' behind the action group which was being formed to address:

'. . . the worst case of military rape in the country. Talking has not got us anywhere. I want to advocate positive action and I have had about 100 letters

'Whose Dorset?' – countryside campaigner at Askerswell in 1972

Left: Rodney Legg's shot of Sea Cottage, Worbarrow Bay, for his new magazine in 1968

from people supporting me. I believe we could muster about a dozen boats with some 50 people for a landing on the shores. I think there is a legal loophole whereby they would be unable to stop us landing. We would, of course, be armed only with banners.'

I opened the proceedings that afternoon with a fighting speech. The core of our case was that that Tyneham parishioners had been dispossessed six days before Christmas in 1943 with the promise that they could return at the end of the war:

'Tyneham is devastated. Its cottages and farms are smashed by shellfire. Many of the evicted now lie in alien cemeteries, and the remainder have re-established their lives elsewhere. So a simple return and a genuine honouring of the pledge is no longer possible. Our answer must be to advocate that this superb stretch of five miles of the finest British coastline – from Lulworth Cove to Kimmeridge – is given to the National Trust. People have a right to visit it. Many have only heard of it from the lucky few who can remember Sunday picnics at Arish Mell, Mupe and Worbarrow during the Thirties.'

Once you have a committee around you, and are holding torchlight processions and taking deputations to see Lord Carrington, and petitions and a wreath into No. 10 Downing Street, the answers are no longer that simple. Peter Carrington seemed to enjoy his time with us, accepting a quality bottle of Spanish sherry and explaining that when asked whether he has one or two 'r's in his name he always spells it out in full:

'S-M-I-T-H. Smith!'

But then, he is an aristocrat. By the time of our first open meeting, at Wareham in November 1968, the ideals of the inaugural meeting had been

Rodney Legg addressing a bank holiday crowd at Tyneham in 1972

compromised. Both main points were trimmed in response to accusations that we were 'flogging a dead horse'. Firstly, we began acting like de facto agents for former landowners and their families, dropping my point about National Trust involvement, and envisaging holiday cottages. Secondly, there was dissent about just what we were fighting to release. Some wanted it restricted to the coastal valley at Tyneham, as this was regarded as a practical objective, rather than all the land that was requisitioned in 1943.

Meanwhile, Lord Nugent had been appointed by the Heath Government to chair a Defence Lands Committee, to review future military requirements. We must have presented a persuasive case, as the resultant green paper decided in our favour, recommending that the Royal Armoured Corps should move from Dorset to alternative tank ranges at Castlemartin in Pembrokeshire. Getting it implemented proved much tougher.

I made a stand on the 'half a pledge' issue in the spring of 1973 and hijacked much of the membership of Tyneham Action Group to form an alternative pressure group. Three other officers resigned to join the breakaway 1943 Committee. The *Daily Telegraph* reported my reservations about the Nugent report, on 6 July 1973, detailing 'grave concern' over the proposed dispersal of the land:

'One of the greatest victories ever won by the conservation lobby in this country will be thrown away to the landowning caucus that controls the Dorset countryside unless we win this new battle. We want the area placed under the National Trust and for it to become a natural reserve. The Department of the Environment has said it will be offered back to the former owners in accordance with the Crichel Down rules. We believe they are making a deliberate misinterpretation of these so-called rules.'

The Sunday Times carried a similar quote on 8 July:

'The real battle is still to come. That is for National Trust ownership of all land released by the Government for amenity and leisure reasons. Otherwise

34

the public is liable to find it has less access rights than it enjoys at the moment from the Army. This is the conservation opportunity of the century and we don't want it lost.'

The new militancy included painting green 'Free Purbeck, Free Tyneham' slogans over red 'Danger, Keep Out' until the Army found an effective solvent for cleaning them. So we then removed the signs for surreal burial into the milky depths of a flooded claypit. Fences were cut, locks wrecked, and trespassing exploits mounted, including a candlelit Christmas carol service. 'Tyneham group dodge police', *Dorset Evening Echo* reported on its front page. Publicity spread on a grand scale, with print and television reports appearing around the globe, from British Columbia to Cape Town and New Zealand.

Retaliation followed in Purbeck. Iconic cottages which we had been photographing for propaganda purposes were demolished by the Army. 'If we were in Northern Ireland, I would shoot you!' said a sergeant with wild staring eyes, as I passed him after we had cut our way through barbed-wire beside Tyneham church. Lulworth residents produced their own posters:

'Locals say "Legg Off!" Our work, our homes. Army to stay.'

Parliamentary allies had to be shown the position on the ground but as a matter of stubborn principal we refused to request permission to visit. Fenner Brockway who I had heckled in a previous existence was now Lord Brockway, our spokesman, in the House of Lords. Born in 1888, he had to be excused trespassing exploits, but enthusiastically agreed to the suggestion that I drove him across the ranges, on along the rough track from East Lulworth to Creech, in my Morris 1100. I had a stolen key to the padlocked gates. En route we showed him 'the biggest hole in Dorset' – 75 feet deep and a quarter of a mile wide – created by open-pit mining of ball clay, inside the permanent no-go area. It had functioned for two decades without planning permission though an embarrassed Dorset County Council then granted retrospective consent.

Fenner Brockway recalled that day in his autobiography *Towards Tomorrow* in 1977:

'Somehow they got hold of a master key which opened all gates and when I visited them they took me on a guided tour, ending with a cheese and wine party round a bonfire on a prohibited hill above the coast. This was the first time since my years as a conscientious objector and my forged passports for refugees from Nazism that I had knowingly broken the law, but the spirit of these young people was so gay and infectious that I could not resist. With Tyneham I fell in love.'

The most bizarre trespassing adventure took place on the sunny morning of Sunday 15 April 1973, when a Member of Parliament, his agent, and myself were chased three miles across downland, along a stream bed and through woodland by 20 soldiers and three Land-Rovers. The entire Tyneham valley was sealed off to the public at that time. Though we were out of condition, we kept giving our pursuers the slip, and left in our own time.

Graham Tope, the Liberal member for Sutton and Cheam, had been staying at the Blackmore Vale hideaway of his agent, Michael Key. Michael and I decided to give Graham a walk in Dorset's wild country. It started ordinarily enough along the ridgeway from Whiteway Hill to Flower's Barrow, where we stood in silhouette looking down over Lulworth Camp and Arish Mell. From there we stumbled and slipped down the smooth grass, skating along on our backsides, towards Worbarrow.

After we had descended 300 feet, being brought to a halt by the ruins of an old barn, we saw there was a problem. Two soldiers were watching us from a Land-Rover parked near the beach. So we changed course, by turning inland along the bramble thickets that skirt the foot of the escarpment, to Baltington, half a mile away. Here I took photographs, until Michael said:

'Come on Rodney, there's another Land-Rover coming down from Whiteway.'

Reinforcements had been radioed from Lulworth. I continued to squint into the viewfinder and could see nothing except the farm. As Michael urged me to hurry, I realised there was a cloud of dust approaching, and that my lingering had given the vehicles several hundred yards additional advantage. The three of us ran due south, past the dark green hulk of a Saladin armoured personnel carrier, and tangled our feet in lines of discarded white wire from manually-guided missiles. A pair of roe deer jumped from the bushes with heart-shaped tufts gleaming from their rumps.

In the trees of Tyneham Gwyle we found a deep-cut bend in the stream bed and lay still, watching the water rippling between the stones, for 15 minutes. Silence returned, so we moved off, and again changed direction. This time we followed the stream up the valley. For 400 yards we crashed, staggered and fell through the trees which were strewn with 30 years of uncleared deadwood.

The decision was taken to boldly go, by leaving the jungle and crossing the main valley track, southwards and seawards across open ground. Just as we were poised to climb the first barbed wire fence, a Jeep appeared, coming up from the bay. We jumped backwards and flung our faces into the stinking wild garlic that smothered the ground. As the truck rumbled by I heard one of the men say:

'We've lost the bastards.'

Immediately it disappeared around the bend, we leapt across the fence, ducked under the wire on the other side, and bounded madly uphill in full view of the entire valley. Michael led the way in a half-mile Olympic sprint that seemed quite likely to launch him off the clifftop. Graham and I strained and pained and then forced ourselves up the last few paces to the cover of an old stone wall.

None of us had looked back but we were sure that we had been spotted and

At home in Milborne Port with Elgar the parrot

Colin Graham, as photographer for Dorset *magazine, pictured by Rodney Legg*

Piggy Legg and Rodney, photographed by Colin Graham

In St Mary's Church marking the 50th anniversay of the eviction of Tyneham villagers, on 19 December 1993, photographed by Sam Rock

Rodney Legg in bed with Piggy, photographed by Colin Graham

that fit professionals would be hurtling towards us with a speed that would make our efforts seem pathetic. As we were in no state to run any further we slumped back against the wall and prepared to give up.

Then as life returned to our bodies we scanned the valley and were amazed to see a party searching the Baltington brambles where we had been nearly an hour earlier. They were a mile away, and had all been looking downwards, as we made our uphill flight. Confidence brimmed and we saw ourselves in the next re-make of *Colditz*. We lay back in smug self-congratulation in the sun, preparing to resume our walk in peace, when the soldiers disappeared.

Instead, a Land-Rover hurtled towards us in full cry, sweeping its path through the deep grass of the ungrazed hillside. Our stone wall was exposed from the side, so we bolted round the back of a blackberry bush and resumed our tactic of lying silent. They passed by, in what must have been a chance sweep.

The moment they were gone we turned east, in and out of view, up the slope from Gad Cliff to Tyneham Cap. We saw one Land-Rover searching Worbarrow hamlet and another with four men who had started to look into and under everything in the Rectory grounds, again the best part of a mile away. The sound of a third Land-Rover came from Tyneham village. They obviously thought we were hiding in one of the ruined buildings. We reviewed the entire manoeuvres from our 500-feet viewpoint.

Again we changed our direction by 90 degrees, for the sixth time since the chase began, and noisily descended through a belt of sycamore, beech and primrose woods to the ruins of the Bond family mansion, confident that our adversaries were making so many sounds of their own that they would never hear us.

The main part of the Elizabethan house was as it had been left after demolition in 1968, but we were surprised to find that at the back, in the older section, workmen from the Environment Department had spent the previous week supporting ceilings, fitting doors and repairing masonry. The original mediaeval wing of Tyneham House was in the process of being restored whilst the ranges continued to be used for tank gunnery; an 'impossibility' that was given in 1968 as the reason for demolition. We were elated as we took it as a physical sign that Tyneham was to be free.

From here, at our own pace, we walked and rested in a northward saunter to the upper reaches of Tyneham's Gwyle stream, through the sheep fields, and then directly up the steep side of the Purbeck Hills. We watched the Land-Rovers pull out along the road, and left the military barbed-wire at the viewpoint on Povington Hill, two minutes after the get-away car had arrived to whisk us to lunch at the Weld Arms in East Lulworth. From there I telephoned the Range Officer to tell them they could stop looking for us – but there was no reply as they were still doing just that.

On one of our deputations to Whitehall, to present a 2,500-name petition to Lord Carrington, the Secretary of State for Defence, on 29 November 1973, we called on the Government to implement the Nugent Report 'provided that this land is handed to the National Trust and conserved with all its exceptional ecological importance'. This we maintained, was in line with the general mood in Purbeck, rather than that articulated by those we called 'Lulworth camp followers' under their banner Keep the Army in Dorset.

Lord Carrrington saw problems with any attempt at fudging the 'Crichel Down rules' which were established when Sir Thomas Dugdale resigned from Churchill's post-war administration. That case, also from Dorset, established the principle that land no longer required for official use had to be offered back to former owners and their heirs. Ironically, as Parliamentary Secretary to the Minister of Agriculture and Fisheries at the time of the Crichel Down scandal, it had nearly ended Peter Carrington's Westminster career before it had started.

At Easter in 1974, having cut through barbed wire fences, we entered the ranges with a spade to plant four iceberg rose-bushes in the churchyard at Tyneham. Soldiers stood by as we filed through, and the reporter George Willey asked me who in the 1943 Committee had been daubing slogans across the ranges:

'I've no idea who painted the signs, but I congratulate them.'

For more respectable activities we called ourselves the Friends of Tyneham. The original Tyneham Action Group, now a model of inaction, disowned 'those creating too much propaganda and publicity'. Describing the Lulworth Ranges as 'Dorset's greatest natural wilderness' we urged the continuation of rough grazing, on the grounds that any more intensive forms of agriculture would 'vandalise and devastate' this unique chain of varying habitats which provide a refuge for many rare and vanishing species of birds, animals, insects and plants. The hedgerows of a complex of little fields around Povington hamlet dated back to Anglo-Saxon times. Grass-grown ridges and furrows across the former open fields of the 3,003-acre parish of Tyneham remained untouched since mediaeval farming methods had been abandoned.

In August 1974, Lord Brockway and Neil Macfarlane MP joined us in a deputation to Lord Brayley, the Army Minister. Our chairman, Mrs Mavis Caver, said it was especially appropriate to ask a Socialist minister to honour the old pledge to return the land, since we were from Dorset which had given the Labour movement its Tolpuddle Martyrs. Brayley, one of Harold Wilson's more inexplicable appointees, first knighted and now ennobled, was bewildered:

'The Tolpuddle Marchers, who were they?'

The following month Brayley resigned over financial allegations and the Government rejected Lord Nugent's recommendations. On 14 September 1974, we were on Beer Head and occupying the seats on an open-air platform to disrupt the official ceremony to open the Devon and Dorset sections of the South West peninsula long distance path. Posters drew attention to the seven-mile gap in the route caused by the Lulworth Ranges. Having delayed proceedings for half-an-hour, we then let Viscount Amory proceed with cutting a tape with scissors, to a timely interjection from Barry Cuff:

'You'll need wire-cutters at Tyneham!'

Tyneham Action Group voted to disband itself (by 88 votes to 69) in November 1974 and as a parting shot sent letters to the three national party leaders. I countered this with telegrams pointing out that despite 'the Government's betrayal' the fight for Tyneham was not yet over:

'This is far from the case as the Friends of Tyneham, with the support of 1,000 members, is still campaigning as vigorously as ever.'

In December 1974, with former resident John Gould, we entered No. 10 Downing Street with a wreath of Tyneham ivy. It came from the garden of ruined Gardener's Cottage where the old soldier was born in 1912. Another wreath, attached to the door of St Mary's Church at Tyneham, was interlaced with barbed wire to symbolise the Army's hold on the ghost village. John Gould was serving with the Devonshire Regiment in India, in 1943, when he heard that his home had been requisitioned. The wreath, which was handed to Prime Minister Wilson's secretary, carried this message:

'To remind those in authority of a broken pledge to the people of Tyneham.'

That, however, was always wishful thinking, as there were no circumstances in which former tenants – unlike freeholders – could been given a right to return to their homes. Sadly, the passage of time has since seen the demise of most of the former residents, though some are at home in Tyneham churchyard. Despite our reservations, the outcome has turned into a remarkable success story, both for nature conservation and public access.

Our Tyneham campaign had been defused by a classic British compromise. The Government decided that the Army could stay, but that the people could walk along the coast path and across the Purbeck Hills, when firing stopped at weekends and block-leave periods for Easter, August and Christmas. Sorting out the details on the ground was put in the capable hands of Brigadier Roy Redgrave, Commandant of the Royal Armoured Corps Centre, who soon found that pleasing everyone is impossible. Ornithologists told him that walkers would scare the birds. Geologists warned that the great British public would leave with chunks of the Fossil Forest. Bureaucrats were fearful of allowing families to walk along unfenced grassy tracks through expanses of ground concealing unexploded shells. Ramblers, as always, asked for more paths. User groups representing campers, caravaners, climbers, horse riders, motorcyclists and surfers sought parity with the walkers.

Each lobby group was resisted in a brilliant burst of applied alacrity. Putting the vision into reality, with a conservation culture that is a model of its kind, has been due to the commitment of Major Mick Burgess and his team of Range Wardens. Writing his military memoirs, Major-General Sir Roy Redgrave recalled in *Balkan Blue* in 2000 that his winning formula had been to circulate minutes with notes to the effect that if no dissenting comments were forthcoming within 48 hours the decisions would be put into effect. He expressed delight that as a 'constant critic' I had been gracious enough to write an enthusiastic editorial headed 'In Redgrave Park' in my *Dorset* magazine. It appeared in October 1975 on the eve of his posting to Europe's divided city, as British Commandant Berlin:

> '*The virtual conversion of a major Army Range from a weekday training ground into a weekend public park has been masterminded by Brigadier Redgrave. He has coped successfully with balancing traditional military activities and new mass access plans. Redgrave, who deserves "Public Relations Officer of the Year Award", leaves Bovington in November.*'

Tyneham has found its historian in Patrick Wright who documented our fight in *The Village that Died for England*. This has expanded in its second edition into a 486-page epic of investigative journalism.

–4–
Buying an Island

Campaigning after Tyneham might have been an anti-climax but I had already moved on to new causes. Some, such as interventions to save the west Dorset wilderness at Powerstock Common from clear-felling and Forestry Commission conifers, were shared with broadcaster and author Kenneth Allsop who deserted Hertfordshire for Milton Mill near Bridport. He was a category one celebrity, instantly recognisable to just about everyone in the country both by sight and sound, as a result of BBC television's *Tonight* programme in the 1960s. Despite having lost a leg, and other health problems, the 53-year-old still looked engagingly youthful when he took his life with an overdose on the depressingly damp morning of 23 May 1973. His last despair had been for the future of the peregrine falcon which had been eliminated through much of its range by egg-failure caused by agricultural chemicals such as dioxins.

Money poured into Lime Grove Studios, particularly from pensioners, with requests for a memorial as a tribute. Many letters contained five shilling postal orders. Film producer John Percival, international author John Fowles, travel writer Brian Jackman, *Food for Free* author Richard Mabey, and composer Andrew Lloyd Webber decided to mount a wider public appeal. The proceeds were to be shared between environmental ginger group Friends of the Earth and a project to buy a nature reserve.

That was where I came in. As editor of *Dorset*, I was enlisted to find that special place. Our first target, appropriate in every way, was Eggardon Hill above Powerstock where Ken went birdwatching. In the event, soaring land prices spiked our bid, and it became clear that Dorset County Council was going to ensure that the National Trust would acquire the Iron Age hill-fort viewpoint.

'Have you thought of looking in a different Channel?' land agent Nigel Murray asked me on 10 September 1973. 'Would you like to consider an island?' He told me that Baroness Wharton wanted to sell Steep Holm to a conservation body but had been rejected by the established charities. The National Trust steered clear of the 50-acre rock in the middle of the Bristol Channel after John Cripwell from Stourhead encountered 'insurmountable access difficulties'. John Fowles, in particular, rose to the challenge. After we visited the island on the grey day of 4 November 1973 – each for the first time in our lives – he told us that Eggardon, in contrast, would have been 'a green gravestone'. Ken, he thought, would 'somehow still be alive on Steep Holm, purely because it is a challenge, it does need work and energy and people to love it and take it in hand'.

The outcome was that we were given authority to manage the island, as if we owned it, while fund raising went on. The freehold price was a quite reasonable £25,000. Baroness Wharton, who had spent her life providing free veterinary services for ill-kept pets in Portugal, died in May 1974. She was succeeded by her daughter, the Honourable Mrs Myrtle Olive Felix 'Ziki' Robertson (1934-2000), wife of composer Harry McLeod Robertson.

Ziki not only honoured the previous agreement but said that whatever the balance currently in our bank account it would be acceptable to her. It was with some embarrassment on our part that the Kenneth Allsop Memorial Trust bought Steep Holm in 1976 for a give-away £10,000 (the price of a semi-detached house in Ealing). Ziki, a campaigner for animal rights in the House of Lords, became vice-president of the RSPCA. An extraordinarily bubbly character, remembered in the Palace of Westminster for in-house photography, she died from Creutzfeldt-Jakob disease.

It became my great adventure, for 25 years, organising boat trips to Steep Holm through and between the gales of a consistently windy part of the century. The six miles of turbid water between Weston-super-Mare and the island experience a rise and fall of the tide second only to that of the Bay of Fundy in Canada. The delightful chocolate-brown colour of offshore Somerset comes from silt in suspension; just one part in 4,000 to be precise, as ascertained by instruments I put down for the Hydraulics Research Station.

We started out in a motorised rowing boat, the *Jane*, and soon learnt that the boating timetable had to slot around tides that climaxed with a rise and fall of 42-feet twice a day. Optimum landing times are an hour and a half before high water or a similar time after the tide has turned. Waiting around offshore, for the moment when the water stops surging across the only beach, is also par for the course. Sometimes we were forced to nose into the rocky remains of the Victorian South Landing. Other times the weather won and we were forced to head for home after a re-enactment of the Battle of the Atlantic.

Calm but foggy days also proved memorable. Mid-morning on 17 April 1976 the erect, five feet high, pointed back-fin of an adult male killer whale (*Orcinus orca*) emerged from a bank of mist, on the starboard side of our small blue boat. This was packed with day-trippers and we had overshot the island in the fog. The animal, which must have been 25 to 30 feet long, was in the deep-water shipping lane about a mile-north west of Rudder Rock. It was us who should not have been there.

That day the island was a needle in the proverbial haystack and we resorted to following the gulls to their nests. In the process we were nearly run over by the *Balmoral* steamer and a large tanker. 'This is like a Conrad novel', Colin Graham said. My lasting impression is of looking up at that tanker, being unable to see either its bow or stern, which were in the fog. Between them, seemingly in slow motion, a seaman walked the length of the ship. Then it was gone. At little later boatman Ian Watts had to contend with its convulsive wake.

On the island, often stranded for longer than they expected, we received a succession of work parties in an endless project to renovate an extensive Victorian barracks dating from Lord Palmerston's fear of involvement and invasion during the Franco-Prussian War. Associated war-works include barbettes for 7-inch rifled cannon, nine out of ten of which have their original 7-ton gun barrels lying in situ (the ninth being found with a metal-detector). Overlapping these are the concrete remains of batteries for 6-inch anti-ship guns and 40-mm Bofors anti-aircraft artillery emplaced in 1941 as part of the Fixed Defences Severn to protect the convoys arriving from America. Rusting steel and plastic-armour canopies have been largely removed by explosives and hard labour in the name of health and safety.

As warden I was the guardian of two disappearing botanical rarities, the stunning wild peonies and original mediaeval stock of wild leeks as introduced by Augustinian monks. The former were found to thrive when seed was removed to the sunny 250-feet summit, away from cliffside crags shaded by a sycamore wood. The latter turned out to produce infertile seed, so could only be propagated from their bulbs, and over the centuries these had trickled down the cliff into the splash-zone. They simply needed taking back to the top.

Ironically, the peregrine falcons over which Ken Allsop had despaired, recovered in numbers along the western seaboard and by the end of the decade were breeding again on our precipitous northern cliffs. The cormorant colony, the only one on this coast, was also thriving. Tony Parsons, a naturalist from Crewkerne, ringed migrating birds and proved that the island plays an important role in spring and autumn.

The bird for which the island is notorious was the herring gull. Having inherited 10,000 pairs, sustained by the refuse culture of open tips on mainland England and Wales, we initially balked at the filth and disturbance to other species. Then disease intervened and thousands died with avian botulism from food putrefying in the anaerobic conditions created by ubiquitous use of black plastic rubbish sacks. The species against which I could only envisage constant warfare was now itself endangered.

My personal obsession was rebuilding old stone walls. That took practical form at the Inn above the beach – blown up by the Royal Engineers in 1941 when they constructed a cable-operated incline railway up the cliffs – which is now once again a usable building. Christopher Somerville found me wall-building when he arrived to research *The Other British Isles* which was published in 1990:

'Most of these wartime buildings are scheduled monuments of one kind or another. They all need to be preserved, and I feel it's a sort of duty to the men who built them to maintain them properly. But where do the priorities lie? There are six Victorian batteries on the island, ten guns, several World War Two searchlight posts, generator housings, Nissen huts – all in disrepair. Then there's the priory ruins being excavated, the farmhouse and walled garden falling to pieces on top, the cottages and the old inn here, which we're hoping to do up as a better warden's house than the barracks. Visitors have to be kept safe, too; one old man gashed his leg badly, falling down the steps by the

Rodney Legg and Colin Graham (both in the water) helping visitors to walk the plank from the Weston Lady *in 1982*

Above, left: *Warden Rodney Legg (centre) making a lesurely departure in the* Jane *with boatmen Ian (right) and John Watts, photographed by Colin Graham;* Middle: *Playing with the sea aboard the improvised* Guano *raft;* Right:*Jenny Smith (left) and Chris Maslen to the rescue as Rodney Legg is washed up on the rocks*

Posing with a botulitic seagull

Sheets of Steep Holm stamps with printers Brian Nicholson and Stephen Taylor, photographed at Gillingham, Dorset, by Colin Graham

beach, so those had to be replaced. And this wall – it's to stop visitors falling over on to the rocks. That's a sample of the repair work, but on top there's the wildlife to be managed – birds, plants, the Muntjac deer I brought over a few years ago. Steep Holm is wonderful for birds – we have peregrines nesting here, and you'll have seen the gull nests everywhere.

'This kind of project needs money as well as voluntary help. We rely entirely on the visitors and their landing fees. We get no government grants of any kind. The Allsop Memorial Trust members, thank goodness, are wonderful with their help and labour. They come and stay on the island – people who prefer to do rather than to talk. The whole place would be self-funding if we didn't have such a surfeit of buildings to maintain. As it is, with all the emergency things that need doing as they crop up, it's hard to stick to any proper plan.'

Getting visitors on to the island was only half the problem. The fun part was getting them off again. Even when we were invaded by up to a thousand at a time from the *Waverley* paddle-steamer or *Balmoral* pleasure cruiser, they had to be decanted one at a time via a shuttle service of little boats. Then they walked the plank from the bow into the splash zone of the beach or on to the stub of a stone pier at our South Landing. That was only one stage away from the days that turned difficult and saw us manhandling them up or down over the side like sacks of potatoes. In theory we only landed the punters if we were reasonably sure we could get them off later. Unfortunately the weather often had other ideas.

The closest that Steep Holm came to being the lead item on *News at Ten* came on Monday 27 June 1983. The *Waverley* disgorged an estimated 700 visitors and crew on the island in the middle of the day. The *Weston Lady* ferried them ashore at the rate of 60 at a time. Some had come from Weston but the bulk were picked up in Penarth, which had been the *Waverley's* last port of call. The excessive interest was due to a combination of a newly refitted ocean-going steamer and the mystery of an island visible but so remote to those living on the Welsh coast. Few boats had landed from there since the island had been de-militarised in 1944. And this was a 'nice' day.

The *Waverley*, however, turned into the ultimate example of the British love for queuing. There were queues for everything, each intersecting other queues, as everyone queued for something – coffee, snacks, souvenirs and the toilets. The entire boat became an immobile throng of humanity. Off Steep Holm they also queued for out.

That exit, to cross the final few hundred yards to our beach, turned out to be relatively painless but on the island they resumed queuing. Hundreds lay siege to the Barracks and our own inadequate water-closets where they soon blocked the drains. Strangely there were sections of the island path network that remained empty as people clustered around our limited 'facilities' in an amorphous biomass. They spent well on the island's privately-printed postage stamps. One man expressed disappointment at our otherwise limited offerings:

'Where is the craft shop that we were told about on the boat? I collect a commemorative tea-spoon from everywhere I visit.'

Disembarkation started at 14.30 hours. This first boat-load was told they had to go back on the *Waverley* at 16.30. Their collection from the beach seemed to take an age. The wind had picked up and then the tide began to turn. The *Weston Lady* had to make numerous attempts to come alongside the steamer. Then she had to break-off as the swell lifted her into the side of the big boat's paddle-box. I realised things were going slowly but the first indication I had of real problems was when a group of people I had loaded on to the *Weston Lady* an hour-and-a-half before were spotted coming up the path on to the island. A lady told me:

'We couldn't get to the **Waverley**. *Your boat was being thrown up and down by the waves. So he had to eventually give up and bring us back to the beach.'*

I asked if it was just her party that had been left stranded.

'God, no! There are hundreds. The beach is full of people.'

I went on to Tower Rock and looked down. It was like the Dunkirk evacuation without the sand or any boats. Water was breaking across the beach. Spray blew ashore as the tips of the waves spumed in the freshening wind. One man wore an ultra-large 'PS *Waverley*' T-shirt with a picture of the boat I could no longer see. Ours was also gone:

'Waverley's gone to Penarth to pick-up an evening cruise and your boat's back at Weston to get some more beer.'

The sun had gone from the beach and the dispirited mass was beginning to realise it had been abandoned. I ran to the Barracks to unpack and unlock – it had been closed as we too prepared for home – and the mob were in close pursuit. Panic buying followed of everything – all the remaining drink, chocolates and Pot Noodles. No one dared estimate the number of people on the island; it ran into hundreds. A tall stern-faced man collared me:

'I must get word to my school. You must have an emergency telephone. There's a coach waiting for us.'

All I could offer was a citizen-band radio. Much to my surprise the lads managed to bring it to life (there had been some problem with the aerial) and then penetrate the inanities ('Cherokee Chief calling Serbonian Temptress for an eyeball'). Somehow, through the language of the primeval slime, they made contact with a thinking Neanderthal.

As for the other facilities, the toilets remained blocked and the sum total of the island's bedding amounted to 18 old mattresses. Warmth came from hastily demolished elder bushes that were made to fit, rather reluctantly, into two small grates. Artificial light was limited to a handful of candles. Emergency food comprised a dozen boxes of rusty catering-size tins of kidney beans, celery and spinach soup. What transpired was told to the *Weston Mercury* by Mrs Edna Murphy of Bleadon, who was far kinder to us than the male callers who found my telephone number from the other side of the Bristol Channel:

'I wondered if we were going to return at all. It looked as though we would have to spend the night on the island.'

It was dusk by the time the last load of visitors had been plucked from the beach by the *Weston Lady* and returned to the *Waverley*. By then the tide had almost completed its cycle and most of the beach had been under water for hours. There was little of it left, as Mrs Murphy explained to the reporter:

'We got off the island quite late in the evening – and by the time we did only a few feet of the beach could be seen. Everybody got off all right, but it was a close-run thing and a tricky operation to manage. The crews of both the **Weston Lady** *and the* **Waverley** *were wonderful. The people from the trust who run the island were also marvellous. It was quite a day.'*

In the *Waverley*, Captain David Neil gave the order to weigh anchor as the paddles turned and the silhouette of a depopulated island was put behind us. There was a call on the paddle steamer on the marine radio from Swansea Coast Guard:

'Captain Neil, just to let you know there's press and television waiting for you when you get back to Weston.'

He stayed on the bridge at Weston-super-Mare and the trust's party of helpers slipped off amongst the last of the contingent of English visitors, via John Watts's *Weston Lady*, for the final hundred yards into Knightstone Causeway. The Welsh parties would be home too late to hear what was now the first item on the brief late-night news summaries. The nightmare turned into a celebration. It was the first time the trust would bank a four-figure sum from a single day's boating. The bag was bulging and I did a quick calculation:

'Yes, we've done it. It's over a grand!'

Later strandings on the island involved fewer people but were often marked by a disproportionate sense of panic. Fear of isolation is a hair-trigger for mass hysteria. The 'Emergency Shelter Fund' tin which I used to rattle around the homeward boat collected a total of £850 for the trust in the 1980s. It did particularly well in the close-run exits where we just managed to beat the elements. It was used to buy 50 sleeping bags to go with bunks and mattresses purchased through help from the Countryside Commission and Woodspring District Council. There were also three cases of decent claret so that civilised values could be maintained. Psychological needs are less easily serviced.

In those far off days before mobile phones, the withdrawal syndrome set in as stays on Steep Holm exceeded 24 hours, inducing an irrepressible (deliberate pun) desire for media attention. One's suffering and eventual return – an event which recedes with every tide – had their counterpart on the mainland where grieving relatives reached for the telephone.

'Island Rescue' and 'CB Rescue' the *Sun* and the *Star* reported on 25 April 1985. The latter was fractionally more informative than that of the competition:

'Twelve wildlife enthusiasts, stranded for four days by storms on Steep Holm island in the Bristol Channel, were rescued yesterday after a CB fan picked up their SOS.'

None of the reports bothered to spoil the story by saying that for three of those four days the party had been booked to stay on the island. In getting through the additional unscheduled night they had rummaged through our emergency stores and caused me to lose my last reminder of the summer of 1982. Someone knew their wine. They found and drank my best bottle of that vintage despite a label proclaiming it was my personal property, not for sale, laid-down for ten years to mature.

Sometimes visitors did not stay long enough to be stranded. Peter de Ionno filed this story for the *Western Daily Press* of 22 June 1981:

'Noises in the night and ghost stories terrified two teenage girls alone on a deserted island in the Bristol Channel at the weekend. Jane Williams and Vicky Phillips, both aged 16, had to be rescued by lifeboat during their first night on Steep Holm island bird sanctuary.'

It was hardly night, however, for at 20.00 hours that Saturday it was still light. The girls sent up a distress flare. A passing yacht alerted the Coast Guard and Weston lifeboat was launched. John Watts, our own boatman, found the pair stumbling down the rocky path to South Landing. They said they were so terrified that they had been thinking of swimming home to Penarth. Vicky then fell over, tearing her jeans and gashing her knee, so she returned with a large scar 'as a souvenir'.

Earlier in the day our work party had told them the story of the island's legendary ghost – St Gildas from the sixth century – and the girls insisted they had heard footsteps crunching the non-gravel surface of the path outside the Barracks. Noises-off certainly included shrieking from the seagulls and probably the barking of Muntjac deer, deep in the undergrowth, at dusk. As they retreated indoors they failed to come to terms with a huge, dark building, without any electricity at that time. The combination made for utter terror.

It led to questions about the wisdom of allowing young people to stay on the

*Rodney Legg (left) and Tim Wike in
rebuilt 'Level 3' of the Inn on Steep Holm*

*Chris Maslen (left) passing a bucket of
mortar for Jenny Smith to hand to Rodney
Legg on top of the west wall at the Inn*

*Excavating 'Level 1' of the Inn with Rodney
Legg (right) and Andrew Buncombe,
photographed by Colin Graham*

*The Inn on Steep Holm, midway through
rebuilding, photogrphed by Rodney Legg*

*Legg on the Rock, exuberant on
completing the east wall at the Inn*

*Left: Rodney Legg wall-building,
photographed by Colin Graham*

island alone. In this case the girls had been brought by their parents, and parted with the day visitors, having pleaded for them to be allowed to stay for the weekend. Lone males were liable to present us with similar problems. The previous week one wannabe Robinson Crusoe had a virtual mental breakdown on being brought back from his self-imposed isolation. Another, a climber in his twenties, disowned his companions and insisted on tackling our crumbling cliffs entirely on his own. I found him dangling with unsecured ropes, almost comatose, after having experienced a fit. After I pulled him to safety he collapsed against a wall. His explanation:

'I was prussuking to overcome my vertigo.'

Our best ever passage boat was the steel-plated *Ivanhoe* which had been a ship's lifeboat aboard the Shaw Savill liner *Ocean Monarch*. Her strengths and versatility, and the endurance and skill of boatman John Watts, were tested to the full against heaving waves and a sub-zero wind factor on 9 March 1985. This time citizen-band enthusiast Paul Mason relayed the distress message from Bath Probation Service whose lads, on the island for community service, were running out of supplies after what had become a long weekend.

Conditions were deteriorating. Though soaked and 'shrammed with the cold' before we even ventured out of Weston Bay, we persevered for more than three hours in the face of constant spray and an icy north-western gale. At times, ascertaining our position from Flat Holm Lighthouse with background landmarks on the Welsh mainland, I helpfully pointed out that we were not only failing to make headway but were now travelling backwards.

Arrival was just as bad as *Ivanhoe* heaved up and down in a swirling mix of waves and pebbles. The boys and their leaders, flinging themselves towards us and into the sea, had to be hauled aboard and propelled on to the deck. I thrust my hands over one chap's nose and glasses as he slid in front of me. The turning of the high-sided boat was dramatic. Hereon we sped forwards. The bows heaved out of the water as we surfed the tops of the waves. From beneath us came the recurrent thud of compressed air being trapped under the hull. Half-dead from the cold, the boys expressed their relief:

'We were desperate. I won't tell you what I've just offered to do for the last cigarette on the island.'

Another emergency evacuation was carried out by veteran boatman Frank Watts when the weather suddenly deteriorated as he was taking a routine trip for holidaymakers around Weston Bay. Seriously bad weather forecast for France had suddenly shifted direction and was coming straight towards us. Frank carried out a skilful rescue through mountainous waves but his intrepid actions were not appreciated by the hijacked day-trippers. Several were vomiting over the side as the *Ivanhoe* revolved like a cork. 'I wish I was dead', uttered by a poor lady retching on the deck, were the first words I heard. Strangely, though we had been in the grips of the oncoming depression, Weston Bay remained deceptively sunny as the boat returned to the mainland.

For me the closest that discomfort came to drowning was in 1980. A wave had caught *Ivanhoe*'s side whilst we were loading and tossed her sideways on to beach. The sea crashed broadsides across her fenders and threatened to roll her over. I moved seawards of the bow in a pathetic attempt to haul the *Ivanhoe* clear as I tugged at the painter – the mooring rope – until I fell into the undertow of a huge wave and was washed outwards.

The full predicament did not come home to me until years later when Cheddar quarryman Mike Webber found a snapshot he had taken. It showed me floating like a bag of rags – clinching identification – behind the boat. Jenny Smith, the partner of Chris Maslen who ably succeeded me as warden, then told me that she had dragged me ashore. My only recollection is from the next stage as I lay on the pebbles and watched in what seemed to be slow-motion as boatman John Watts heaved a heavy rope through an eye-ring in semi-submerged rock as waves broke around him.

Others hauled with him and they somehow refloated the boat but with dents and scrapes to the hull that would have proved terminal had she been constructed of ubiquitous modern fibreglass. As for me, back in Weston, I was mothered by the splendid Italian ladies of the Pescara Pizzeria in St James's Street. I was compelled to shed those soaking rags. I was disappointed to have to return the borrowed clothes to their sons, a week later, as there has been no hope for my sartorial image ever since.

Another near miss was the time that an ordinary pick-up turned into a nightmare as we made for home through what the boatmen euphemistically called 'the South Patches roll' in the days when a buoy marked its dangerous shallows. *Ivanhoe* lurched sideways to the left as the sea engulfed the wheel-house and propelled everything inside – ashtray, coins, compass, matches and mugs – into a horizontal shower of debris. Waves continued to smash across us. In minutes the scale of the sea had magnified into peaks and troughs that were house-sized. The dips were big enough to swallow all view of the mainland.

The wild sea ruled out any chance of landing at Weston-super-Mare and as the only alternative we headed towards the semi-sheltered north side of Brean Down. Birdwatcher Dave Reid used his Zeiss binoculars to make out the wisps of willow branches that mark the winding channel into the Axe estuary. Grey walls of mud were momentarily visible and then inundated by the next great wave. Each one surged across half a mile of mudflats to offshore Black Rock reef. We had to edge our way to safety in the narrows towards Uphill.

On land the severity of the gale was even more apparent. First it was blown sand and the effort required for hunched-back walking into town. That seemed to take for ever. Then, beside Beach Lawns, the metal panels from a line of bus-shelters burst their rivets and scudded at knee-level across the road. It was an awesome demonstration of the power of the wind.

Autumn gales, on 19 September 1981, would claim our beloved *Ivanhoe*. Having executed a perfectly timed pick-up, she lifted us off the island and brought

52

us to the lee shore of the Victorian pier at Birnbeck Island, shortly before the full fury of the weather erupted. As she was anchored, for what would be the last time, the size of the seas was visibly swelling. Later that evening the combination of low atmospheric pressure, rising tide, and gusting wind piled up such a volume of water under the boat that she snapped her mooring rope. Next morning she was found wedged in the rocks, up-channel on Sand Point and made her final television appearance. The hull that had withstood a pummelling from beach pebbles was fatally twisted and peppered with fractures. She would be floated home but only for scrap.

Her successor, *Weston Lady*, was similar in shape but had a fibreglass hull. That the 1980s treated her tenderly was due to the seamanship of our boatmen and the greatly improved accuracy of coastal weather warnings. Satellite pictures and computerised interpretations have brought a precision – the odd 1987 hurricane excepted – that compels respect and observance.

Uncomfortable memories of Steep Holm visits sometimes surfaced on the mainland. In 1984, Woodspring Leisure and Tourist director Clive Jackson asked his committee if they were willing 'to risk a fact-finding trip' to the island. Councillor Mrs Mary McEwan-Smith recalled the 'terrible crossing' of a previous occasion:

> *'I got soaking wet on the journey. The boatmen said they had never lost a passenger and I said there was always a first time. You have a job to get on the island because of the beach, and the Barracks are terrible. I think we should spend money on it!'*

Her colleagues endorsed that charitable suggestion and voted us a grant of £1,000, since renewed and increased, which would later be augmented by National Lottery and other public funds.

One of the island's near misses for Channel shipping took place in the mid-1980s when a captain ignored his Admiralty chart and cut across the shingle spit off the beach. It was towards high water and she passed about 150 feet from the shore but there was insufficient depth for the manoeuvre. A largish vessel, coming up the Bristol Channel, had gone right instead of left of the obstacle marked as 'Steep Holm'. Whatever the cause of the miscalculation she had hit the shingle at a right-angle and gouged a trench three feet deep that ran across the spine of the central part of the gooseneck. Some exceedingly large boulders, weighing several hundredweight, had been pushed sideways.

That was nearly a prize catch for us. Frequently the lesser legions of yachtsmen ignore these turbulent waters at their peril. Many among the fraternity show an inability to understand that when in a calm sea you come across a patch of choppy water it is there because underwater obstacles are disturbing the tidal momentum. Normally a grounding costs them no more than time, waiting to re-float if they do it on a dropping tide, but in one instance it punctured the bottom of George Caney's motor boat from Penarth, and had us transferring his passengers at sea. Other times yacht people ignore the rise and

Wardens Rodney Legg and Chris Maslen path-clearing on Steep Holm, photographed by John Pitfield

Helicopter of 707 Royal Naval Air Squadron moving a cannon for the guard-piece beside the island Barracks

Rodney Legg (left) with young visitors helping to clear the firing-hole in the cannon, photographed by Philippa Bowkett

Rodney Legg and Alex Bowkett, celebrating arrival of the 24-pounder Georgian cannon in front of Steep Holm Barracks, photographed by Philippa Bowkett

John Pitfield carrying out the first firing of the obsolete gun barrel since the Napoleonic Wars, photographed by Rodney Legg

force of the turning tide and lose an anchor or even their craft.

An unmanned yacht floated upstream from the island but fortuitously for two despairing Welshmen, screaming from the island beach, our own boat happened to be approaching. She picked us up and pushed upstream in pursuit. It was only as the yacht was about to run aground off Sand Point that we were able to grab it. We were all thoroughly soaked in the process.

The boatmen asked £7 for their trouble but yachtsmen take the precaution of never carrying cash. Experiences, however, are never wasted, and apart from advising the boatmen to take an Open University course in the law on marine salvage, I henceforth discouraged any heroics in the cause of saving property. In 1987 we watched helplessly from the Inn as a rotund gentleman nearly drowned in the tide-race whilst failing to recover a beach-ball.

The drone of an approaching Westland Wessex helicopter used to foretell disaster. Their last operational role was for air-sea rescue. One provided the lesson about not underestimating these waters when she spent the morning checking out the wreckage of the *Amanda Kay* which was floating past the island. The yacht had broken-up between Steep Holm and Flat Holm, possibly after hitting a rock or floating wood, though strong seas can also feel like a solid obstacle.

The search for three or four bodies went on for several days until they became bloated and were washed ashore. The single survivor made his landfall on the other side of Bridgwater Bay at Hinkley Point. On that occasion we talked to the helicopter via radio telephone but it was the only emergency during which the technology worked. In 1987 I was appointed an Auxiliary Coast Guard for the purpose of communicating with their Swansea command centre on the service's Channel-O marine band. Swansea Coastguard sent the Barry Lifeboat, supported by an inshore boat from Weston, to rescue a large party of naturalists in 1992. Conditions deteriorated during the day and they had to wait for several hours beside rock-pools in a biting wind before the operation was mounted at dusk and into the night.

Spectacular exits are passe. It is much more unusual for anyone to arrive in dignity and style. Sometimes I had to leap into a cleft in the rocks at South Landing and alternatively pull the boat in as the water ebbs and then push her seawards as the next wave comes in. That, however, is hardly a dignified entrance for the visitors as they are helped over the bows and then have to scale the rocks and a scree-slope. Ordinarily, the beach landing is uneventful with a simple walking of the plank down on to the pebbles, though even that can have some young males trembling.

The most athletic and unashamedly macho entrance to the island in modern times was 'Operation Sweetholm' in 1976 which was arranged for me by Major Jim Bilton of 25 Field Battery of 19 Field Regiment Royal Artillery, based at Larkhill on Salisbury Plain. He had just run the endless permutations of the computer programme to see if NATO's central front was still defensible and turned his attention to invading Steep Holm for the day. I don't think I had told anyone; certainly not our chairman who stood at the bow with his binoculars, scanning

Rodney Legg greeting eminent natural history photographer Heinz Sielmann, on arrival at Weston-super-Mare, in 1990

for wild leek flower-heads and the outreach of a peregrine from the cliffs to protest our arrival.

Major Bilton's men were behind us, converging on our boat from both sides, in high-speed inflatables. They zoomed in front of our bows as we came into the beach. 'What on earth's going on?' John Fowles asked. 'Just a little welcome for you', I said. At that moment, two Lockheed Hercules transport aircraft of the Royal Air Force came from the north-east, at height over the island. 'Watch the first plane', I told John. 'The parachutists should drop any second.'

'Oh, what have you done?' he sighed. The remark about the paratroops was my little joke but John Fowles remained tense for the rest of the day. As we walked on to the top of the island at Tombstone Battery, a wiry young man with camouflaged face and combat jacket emerged from the bushes in front of us. 'Good morning, sir', he addressed Major Bilton. 'I thought I would come the direct way up the cliffs.'

About the only subsequent entrance to the island to upstage the day of the Army games came in 1987 when Rose Sparrow, from Uphill, literally leapt into our lives. She became the auxiliary tea-lady, a highly important island post, on that first day. Initially, however, we wondered what had descended upon us. Rose, it transpired, had missed the boat. Not being short on initiative she then persuaded the boatmen to take her out to Steep Holm on a later bay-trip that was not scheduled to land. In fact, when they arrived at the island there was such a strong force of tide running across the beach that it was impossible for the boat to come in – we saw from the Inn that they had given up an approach attempt and were backing off.

On the bows, however, there was a woman. She was physically struggling with the older boatman – John 'Kenny' Watts senior – as his son, John Watts junior, reversed the boat out of difficulty. 'You can't do that!' Kenny yelled. She did! The female dropped off the bow with billowing skirts, bolt upright and straight into several feet of water as they continued to edge away from the beach. The figure then flung herself into the waves and splashed the final 40 feet to the beach. The Sparrow had landed.

An out of season visit to the island followed the leak of an estimated 6,000 gallons of oil from Llanwern steelworks, near Newport, in February 1991. The slick had left a tide-mark around the island where we discovered oiled-covered seaweed and dead cormorants. Visible numbers on the cliffs were down from an expected 200 to only 40 birds. That species suffered most because they dive beneath the waves to feed on fish and other marine life. The decline of the herring gull was also at its nadir, from pest-proportions of 10,000 in the 1970s, to only 100 pairs, though their demise had been confirmed as avian botulism, a poison picked up when the birds scavenge on rubbish tips.

The oil-slick coincided with Nanny State catching up with our self-sufficient water supply. Chris Rundle, in the *Western Daily Press* of 11 February 1991, recalled its distinctive taste:

'It may not have the tongue-clinging sparkle of Perrier or the distinctive palate of Malvern, but the water on Steep Holm certainly has character.'

That came from a combination of charcoal filtration and what I described as 'colossal quantities' of coliform bacteria from bird droppings:

'You cannot actually taste the droppings – not that I know what they taste like anyway – and although the water is a sort of murky brown colour that's because it goes through a carbon filter. We always boil it before we use it but a lot of visitors actually like the taste.'

Government regulations were being introduced to monitor private water supplies. Ours was bound to fail the test – and be declared 'non-potable' – with the result that we would have to import it from the mainland and hike the price from 40p to £1 per cuppa. We were also taken to task for illegally selling alcoholic drinks but I rescued that tradition by going legitimate and obtaining a licence from Weston-super-Mare magistrates.

The days of intrepid visitors were about to fade into memory. It still amazes me that we got away with such a catalogue of risks for so long. Our first casualty requiring an Air-Sea Rescue helicopter was Tim Wike from Wincanton who I had been bringing to the island since he was aged eight in 1986. His foot was crushed when a two-hundredweight rock slid down the eastern cliffs on 20 April 1991. The yellow helicopter from RAF Chivenor took him to Cardiff Hospital where his toes were repaired.

'Isle warns: No wimps' Darren Bane wrote in the *Bristol Evening Post* on 10

Homeward-bound in the Weston Lady, *photographed by Colin Graham*

June 1992 and quoted me giving my annual report to the Allsop Trust:

'No wimps is the shortest phrase that says it all. For years we have been describing the island as suitable for the active elderly. But it is time we reminded people that visiting this offshore rock can be a misadventure in a hostile environment. Emergency incidents are increasingly frequent. Last year we had an injured boy lifted off by helicopter and in May this year a party of stranded visitors evacuated by two lifeboats. Between times our first aid room has seen a succession of cuts and bruises from a series of falls.'

Deborah Rundle reported on the May panic for the *Western Morning News* and Jerard Hurst in the *Weston Mercury*. A Force Eight gale gusted out of nowhere with squalls that disrupted a sailing festival in the upper Bristol Channel. Our boat, *Silver Spray*, broke down off the island, and stranded 33 people. Lifeboats and helicopters had rescued up-turned yachtsmen with 13 of them needing hospital treatment. On Steep Holm there were parties from Evesham and Cannington College, Bridgwater, including an 80-year-old woman who collapsed with hypothermia and was also taken to hospital, though the emergency took until darkness to turn into an evacuation. Initially I handed out sleeping bags and began to prepare an evening meal but some visitors went into a state of mutiny:

'The women and children were fine and quite happy about things – but the men started to panic. One had left his children alone in Evesham and was worried they would not be able to cope while others had elderly parents waiting at

home. In the end some were becoming almost hysterical and it was quite difficult to control them. I eventually radioed Coastguards asking for a rescue to be mounted – but was told lifeboats in the area were overstretched by the Portishead incident. Later we saw the 54-foot Arun-class Barry Lifeboat coming in to us. They were joined by the Weston inflatable to ferry us off. The sea was really rough and it was difficult but the lifeboat crews were superb and did a marvellous job.'

Later that year came the annual crop of stinging wasps, lured by visitors leaving half-drunk cans of Coke around and outside the Barracks, sending young adults and their offspring into bouts of localised mass-hysteria. Blackberry time brought another problem with a particular plant with poisonous black berries that had to be enclosed in chicken-wire:

'Yes, it is a deadly nightshade plant immediately outside the door. But it's a botanical rarity and quite harmless provided you don't eat it.'

The island was taking an increasing toll on my energy, health and resources. I provided the April Fool's Day story for the *Western Daily Press* in 1993, with diagrams showing how the island could be hauled sideways along its geological bedding plane, on immense rollers, to take it away from the £10 billion Severn Barrage: The proposal would have moved the island into Bridgwater Bay:

'We never wanted to be that close to the barrage anyway. I've had a look at the site they are proposing and if anything the views are much better from there.'

*Rescue by lifeboat,
photographed by Rodney Legg*

Chris Rundle, the paper's environment correspondent, over-egged the story with clues:

'To avoid further soil erosion, the island will be forested with conifers such as the fast-growing Stapril fir, natural habitat of the Greater Spoofbill, one of the many gulls which flock to the island each spring.'

I then collapsed with nervous exhaustion at Easter, after boating during a bout of flu, and was confined till Whitsun. That was in Ward 9A of Yeovil District Hospital – from which I escaped and walked home, 16 miles through the night – followed by secure accommodation in Tone Vale Hospital, though I was not sectioned under the Mental Health Act. For a time I was manic, to the extent of proclaiming I was Chief-of-Staff of the Provisional Army Council, and saying other nonsense about Northern Ireland that must have been of interest to the Security Service.

On Steep Holm island there was controversy about nude sunbathing which I resolved by both authorising and restricting it to the rocks at South Landing. The island absorbs warmth like a storage heater and this must be the best sun-trap in the Bristol Channel. I'm told it was recommended in David Martin's *Naturist Guide to Britain*. To cater for another request, provision for urn burials was provided in a plot beside the mediaeval Priory.

Subsequently, my Steep Holm regime turned into managed decline, as I planned to opt-out at the end of the century. That would see me 53-years-old and coinciding with Ken Allsop's age at the time of his death. In the event I left earlier, in 1998, after an acrimonious row in which there were attempts to override my insistence that we should never sail with visiting members of the public when there was a gale warning in force for sea area Lundy. Those who succeeded me could never forgive the fact that I went to the papers to defend that fundamental judgment and principle. Me going to the stake for the sake of health and safety? I would never have believed it myself.

–5–
Working with John Fowles

A s an aside from working with John Fowles to find a suitable memorial to our mutual friend Kenneth Allsop, I am credited in Fowles's *Journals* (Volume 2, for 1975) with 'acting in my usual pugnacious way' in having 'fired off letters left, right and centre' in support of Lyme Regis local historian John Oldfield. Oldfield had been blocked by town mayor Henry Chessell from access to a public collection of archive photographs. These were required to illustrate a feature in my *Dorset* magazine which debunked celebrations to commemorate Jane Austen's seaside visits of 1803 and 1804. They could not be copied because the issue was being 'overdone'. On 6 March 1975, Fowles records the upshot:

'This morning Oldfield received a frigid letter from Chessell, arranging a date for the photography. However, Rodney is going to have his pound of flesh: the West Dorset District Council, who finance the museum, have been looking through their files and found that no accounts have been presented under Chessell's curatorship.

'It's made us all laugh. Chessell is behaving more and more like a midden bantam, determined no one else shall share his little literary empire. He has a corner now in guidelets and booklets, all of them merely lifted from [George] *Roberts and* [Cyril] *Wanklyn* [past historians]. *For all his lack of education, Oldfield is ten times more a genuine local historian.*

'A fortnight ago the council voted to erect a plaque on the site of Wings [between the Cobb harbour and Marine Parade], *saying Austen had lodged there. A letter I wrote pointing out the improbability appeared in this week's issue of the* **Lyme Regis News**. *Now Chessell claims he knew this all along, even though he presided over the council meeting of the week before and let the vote go through. He says the matter will be reconsidered.'*

I made sure of that in issue No. 43 of *Dorset* magazine. Three-decker headlines invited a libel writ but none was forthcoming:

'John Oldfield shatters the official preparations for a novelist's bicentenary . . . Councillors make asses of themselves in voting to erect plaque saying Jane Austen lodged in house that was not even built when she saw Lyme . . . An embarrassed Dorset town is told it has got its history wrong.'

*John Fowles (second from right) holding court in the Barracks on Steep Holm,
photographed by Colin Graham*

As well as collaborating on acquisition of the island of Steep Holm, John
Fowles (1926-2005) and I shared an enthusiasm for the words and works of the
seventeenth-century antiquary John Aubrey (1626-97). Together, between 1980
and 1982, we transcribed and published from an incredibly bitty and confusing
manuscript in the Bodleian Library, Oxford, the first edition of his magnum opus
Monumenta Britannica, under the my imprint of Dorset Publishing Company
(partially reprinted by Little Brown in New York). It is the foundation stone of
British archaeology, with the earliest detailed accounts of most of our principal
ancient monuments, and at the behest of Wimborne antiquarian bookseller Bill
Hoade I had taken it upon myself to identify and locate them. John Fowles
became my daily informant and mentor as he corrected slips in deciphering
Aubrey's troublesome handwriting and transcribing its awkward mix of classical
and vernacular language. At an early stage we decided to reproduce a facsimile
of each original page to face our deciphering and interpretation. Other scholars
can attempt their own version of things that seem doubtful.

This refusal to adopt the conventions of normal editing had the advantage of
absorbing rather than abridging Aubrey's quirky anecdotes, asides and insertions
that punctuate the manuscript and its margins. To John Fowles, Lyme Regis author
of *The French Lieutenant's Woman*, Aubrey should be credited – from his acclaimed
Brief Lives – with 'the most pleasing short sentence in the language'. Viz.:

'*I did see Mr Christopher Love beheaded on Tower Hill in a delicate clear day.*'

The brilliance, Fowles maintained, lay in the unexpected use of the word
'delicate'. Extraneous and personal Aubreyisms also pepper his archaeological

offerings. Non-editing was the only way we could avoid throwing out the baby with the bath-water.

Every day I sent John new typings, and he broke off from proper work to decipher, query and return them. All this was done for nothing, though I was able to reciprocate in contemporary kind by giving him – as curator of the town's Philpot Museum on the seafront – the original signed order from King Charles for the siege of Lyme Regis in the English Civil War. I fretted over the phone that he should not be giving such instant prime-time attention to queries that were of so little importance, but to John it was now part of the daily routine:

'It's my therapy for the morning. I do it instead of The Times *crossword.'*

Academics were less than impressed. John Aubrey, himself no archaeologist, was the father of a subject that was yet to have its modern name. John Fowles freely admitted our limitations:

'It may seem appropriate, but hardly recommendable, that this edition has been prepared by two more amateurs. No one knows better than Rodney Legg and myself that in an ideal world the task would have been entrusted to a recognised specialist, or team of specialists, under the aegis of some well-funded university press. But for nearly three centuries now the notebooks have been waiting for this treatment; and have for as long been adamantly left on the shelf. I therefore hope that whatever other accusations are levelled against us, there will not be one of rushing in where angels fear to tread. Rodney Legg, the only begetter of this project, felt that the angels in this case went less in awe of John Aubrey than in sheer terror at the amount of work involved; and I agreed, and offered what assistance I could . . .

'I hope I may finally add that there is one matter over which we will yield to no one: and that is in our regard and affection for Aubrey himself. For both of us this has been a labour of love, a conserving homage to a great conservationist.'

'Big John' (to distinguish him among my surfeit of Johns) had an Orson Welles frame and Solzhenitsyn beard. Verbally, however, he was always so restrained and softly spoken that I could never reconcile the John Fowles of our conversations with John Fowles the novelist. I used to say that it was Elizabeth, his wife, who wrote the books. Hers was the talent for incisive, witty words with perfect delivery. To some extent I was right, as she turned out to have been the catalyst for all John's major work; because after Elizabeth's premature death there were no more novels. His American biographer, Eileen Warburton, quoted me attempting to make this point, for *John Fowles: A Life in Two Worlds* in 2004:

'Rodney Legg always joked that the "ultimate secret" was "Did Elizabeth write the books?", for John Fowles always seemed so busy with other projects.'

Elizabeth was renowned for 'a refreshing lack of reverence toward her famous husband' and the pair of us often conspired to puncture the solemnity of the sycophants who were drawn to him. Interrupting a conversation to say that *Murder on the Orient Express* was John's 'best book' began as a flippant Rodney remark. Elizabeth was quick to adopt it as her own. She also maintained a healthy scepticism when it came to matters concerning 'that bloody island' and frequently stayed ashore after delivering her husband to Weston-super-Mare. She particularly detested the obligatory soakings that accompanied early crossings.

John, on other hand, thrived on it all and explored our rock much like a prepubescent child released for his first school outing into the great outdoors. He wore an old demobilisation-coat with binder-twine for a belt. On returning to civilisation – to treat us to a meal – he began the ritual emptying on to a side-plate of deep pockets that were stuffed with dispossessed purse-web spiders and their condom-like nests, handfuls of colourful banded snails, and whatever unusually shaped or speckled gull egg that he had found during the day.

My average walking speed is often one mile an hour but for John just a hundred yards was not unusual and I would follow his course along the cliffs from a trail of turned-over stones. Physical diversions of the Steep Holm kind and mental challenges like the Aubrey book captivated both John and myself, as Eileen Warburton explained:

> *'Part of the appeal of Steep Holm's remoteness for both Fowles and Legg was that despite an overseeing committee, they actually had free rein and little interference. They both were men of extremely independent mind, not to say downright perversity, and admired this quality in each other. In 1977, for instance, Rodney Legg, entirely on his own authority, introduced hedgehogs and muntjac deer to the island. Fowles was furious at first, mostly because he had not been consulted. He went to Legg's home at Sherborne to confront him, but found "it's impossible to be angry with him . . . he lives in such a mess, cats, animals, two parrots in the lavatory, a shed with lemur-mongooses in the garden; and Rodney himself like some cross between a weasel and a pixie, enjoying the brouhaha". He ultimately defended Legg's action to the more ecologically purist committee members.*
>
> *'Fowles was very aware of how hard Legg worked for so little return. After 1975, when Legg began selling antiquarian books, manuscripts and prints, Fowles became his best customer. Although he loved the rare old volumes, Fowles also bought from Legg in great quantities "to thank him tacitly for all his work for the trust". Legg treasured a note Fowles enclosed with a payment: "Get thee behind me, Satan of Sherborne – decided last week to stop buying so many books, just never get round to reading most of them." However, he finished, "Cheque enclosed . . . have always wanted it in fact".'*

Eventually both John and I did grow out of acquisitive book collecting and for precisely the same reason. To quote John once again:

> *'I need books like a hole in the head.'*

John Fowles (left) and Rodney Legg
exploring the cliffs on Steep Holm,
photographed by Colin Graham

Right: *John Fowles reading* The Times,
photograped by Colin Graham

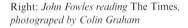

Ironically we will have both ended up bequeathing houses stuffed full of half-read books for others to cherish (or pass on to Charles Cox for erudite cataloguing).

In July 1983, when providing the John Fowles taxi service, my former partner Colin Graham and myself shielded a 'frightened' John from his stalker at Sherborne Station. This 'voluble, neurotic woman' was apparently waiting – along with John – for the next Exeter train on which he was to travel home via Axminster. In his *Journals*, Fowles recorded:

> *'She dresses in a fur-coat, with peculiar harem-type scarlet trousers, tight at the ankle. She has a femme fatale quality that is really sinister: the conviction of her own madness.'*

We gave her the code-name 'Karen'. She had turned up at the door of John Fowles's home – Belmont House above the Cobb in Lyme – and claimed that in a previous life she had been the real-life Sarah Woodruff. Karen, the self-styled 'most beautiful woman in the world', had been an accomplished actress. She was better by half than Vanessa Redgrave who was initially selected to star in the film of *The French Lieutenant's Woman*. Warner Brothers reconsidered but also cheated Karen out of the role and gave it to Meryl Streep. Karen, as a result, was driven to become a street prostitute in the United States:

> *'She says all this with a hypnotically self-contrived blue stare, like a Gypsy door-seller, as if she dares you to believe refusing the white heather will not bring a curse on you. I am as cold as ice, I can't help her; and suddenly it all ends in violent screams. I'm like all Englishmen, I hate women. She walked*

away shouting, 'Shit. Lousy shit!' at the top of her voice, and a distinct threat that I hadn't heard the end of her.'

I don't know what happened to the lady and her obsession but fear of stranger-danger was revived by two incidents a couple of years later. Belmont House was burgled when Elizabeth and John visited America in September 1985. Then it was done over again – much more thoroughly – when they were theatre-going in London in mid-December. Every room and drawer had been thoroughly rummaged but very little had been taken. Real treasures and valuables were ignored. Instead a few 'trinkets' had been removed, as John told me at the time:

'It would have taken an age to rifle through all this stuff. What puzzles me is that they have left so much that obviously had a value. Things have been taken as if they were souvenirs – including those Lyme trade tokens you bought for me at Glendinning's [London auctioneers]. *I never did give you the duplicates I promised. We've also lost my telescope, a clock, calculator and some postage stamps. Liz's cheap camera is gone along with what little jewellery was left from last time. And a chocolate ice-cream from the fridge.'*

Mine was the first tribute to John to appear in the 'Lives Remembered' column of *The Times* on Armistice Day in 2005:

'Throughout his life, the author John Fowles [obituary, November 8] *was a hands-on naturalist. As well as bringing back orchids from France and cuttings obtained in botanical gardens from Tresco to San Francisco, he would stuff the pockets of his bulky old Mackintosh with colourful banded snails and the condom-shaped homes of purse-web spiders. He had a particular fascination for the latter, which he gathered from the rocky slopes of Steep Holm island, which I wardened from 1974 to 1998.*

'John Fowles was our principal paymaster, having enabled the Kenneth Allsop Memorial Trust to buy the 50-acre island nature reserve. On occasions when we were stranded there overnight, six miles off Weston-super-Mare, the situation was hardly helped by John's quietly delivered observation that "gales like this go on for two weeks on the south coast".'

My close friend John Pitfield added his recollections of a visit to Lyme:

'In the mid-1990s Rodney Legg and I collected John Fowles to go to his favourite pub in Lyme Regis. After a convivial evening we walked him back to his house, only to realise that he had not changed out of his slippers for his evening out. Such was the man's relaxed attitude in his Dorset hideaway.'

'Big John' left us in a Bonfire Night gale when the halyards of the yachts beached around the Cobb whistled in unison from just the sort of wind that would have prevented us from either reaching or leaving Steep Holm.

–6–
Mystery of the Mildenhall Treasure

Elizabeth Fowles was a partner in an antique shop across the Devon border in the pretty National Trust village of Branscombe. There I met acquaintances of eccentric retired archaeologist Professor Tom Lethbridge who lived in Hole House until he died at the age of 70 on 30 September 1971. He had departed with a mystery on his mind, as letters and notes confirmed, which lured me to the Fen Country to try and find the true discovery-spot of the Mildenhall Treasure.

Colin Graham and Howard Pell joined in the fun; with Colin to take photographs (we were that hopeful), Howard as our pet archaeologist, and myself as the researcher. Lethbridge had been insistent that nothing should appear in print until half a century after the 'discovery' of those 34 highly decorated items of pagan and Christian Roman silver. It could not to be published until everyone involved – including himself – was safely dead.

Fellow Fenland excavator Gordon Fowler had broken the news that 'a great dish with gods and goddesses rolling all over it' was in police custody at Newmarket. Lethbridge had a double personal interest in the matter since the claimed location coincided with the site of a fourth-century Roman villa – 'a dull little house' – which he excavated with a team of volunteers in 1932. Lethbridge re-entered the story as the 'expert witness' who enabled the coroner to declare the items 'Treasure Trove' – and therefore the property of the Crown – at an inquest held in Mildenhall on 1 July 1946. The verdict relied on Lethbridge's evidence that the silver had been deliberately hidden. It therefore became Crown property with the result that the British Museum acquired it on behalf of the nation.

The silver was found in most unusual circumstances in 1942. The field at West Row, beside Mildenhall Aerodrome, was deep-ploughed during a blizzard for a farmer named Rolfe. The work was done by Gordon Butcher as the employee of contractor Sidney Ford of nearby Thistley Green. Butcher hit the 'Neptune dish' (otherwise called the 'Oceanus dish') with the plough. He did not tell Rolfe the landowner but confided in the discovery with Ford his employer. He acted decisively and fast. Under the cover of the snowstorm the pair of them dug out the remaining treasure just 100 yards from Rolfe's windows.

They hauled their loot in a sack 'another 200 yards or more' to Ford's equipment yard. There Ford cleaned up each piece in his workshop, one at a time, before taking them across the road to display at home on his dresser. Lethbridge

Above, left: *The Mildenhall Treasure, photographed in the British Museum by Colin Graham, stimulated a search for its find-spot*; right: *'Neptune dish' from the Mildenhall treasure trove, two feet in diameter, photographed by Colin Graham*

already knew Ford was a proficient metal worker. He had made the stainless-steel bar that Lethbridge used to prod for underground walls and trenches. Ford would never have mistaken antique silver for 'lead or pewter'.

After the end of the war in Europe, in May 1945, Sid Ford was visited at home by Dr Fawcett, a collector of antiquities, from the Chilterns. Fawcett said he cautioned Ford that he was liable to prosecution for concealing Treasure Trove. What really happened? 'He didn't offer enough', Lethbridge thought. Fawcett left with a 'loose handle' which the British Museum confirmed was Roman silver. Ford then panicked and informed the police who confiscated the hoard and informed the coroner.

To Lethbridge the inquest in the magistrates' court at Mildenhall was 'pure theatre'. Sitting on the dais behind the coroner, he amused himself by comparing the remarkable facial resemblance of Mildenhall policemen, of all ages, one to another.

'"NFN" meaning "Normal for Norfolk" would describe them if we had been in the next county.'

Where was the silver – or pewter – found? Sid Ford drew a map and pin-pointed four places across two fields (it had been snowing at the time). The resultant piece of paper with 'X' to mark the spot disappeared with a hopeful treasure hunter at the end of the day.

Fawcett's most revealing remark was that he remembered 'rather more' items of silver on the dresser than there were at the inquest. Lethbridge was sure that there would have been several jugs. An 'Oxford-voiced' King's Counsel on behalf of Sid Ford told the coroner that it was quite normal for treasure to be lost in the Fens. The significance was that lost objects could not be claimed by the Crown (nor could those in burials such as at Sutton Hoo). It was imperative if the treasure was not to be dispersed or sold at auction and bought by Americans that the coroner's jury found it had been deliberately concealed with the intention of recovery at a later date.

Lethbridge made the key point that farmland at Mildenhall was never part of the watery Fens:

'Things can be lost in Fen peats but not in skirt-land fields which are sand on top of chalk rock and never had any peat on them at all.'

Ford, however, refused to give up. He tried to sue the coroner for wrongful detention of his property but the action was struck off by the High Court because the coroner represented the Crown which could not be sued. The Treasury then refused to compensate the finders the estimated £6,000 'contemporary saleroom value' on the ground that they had hidden the silver for four years.

Sir Thomas Kendrick, who ran the British Museum, insisted on giving Ford and Butcher £1,000. He argued that otherwise future finders would melt down their discoveries.

Meanwhile the informed consensus in London, among those who viewed the treasure, was that it was 'too grand for Britain'. The inference was that it must be war loot, smuggled into RAF Mildenhall from Hitler's Germany or Mussolini's Italy. Coincidentally, two of Sidney Ford's sons-in-law were sergeants serving with the Royal Air Force. They had allegedly flown back from Bari to the big bomber and transport base which was handed over to the United States Army Air Force and continued in its key role through the Cold War.

Lethbridge scrounged a couple of mine detectors, courtesy of the Royal Engineers and Bruce Mitford of the British Museum, who commanded the Dorsetshire Regiment in 1939 and was seconded to the Special Operations Executive. They found that Ford's 'find spot' had been salted with a selection of Roman and Georgian silverware. This made for 'an unlikely combination'. To their audio distress, the rest of the field yielded a fine crop of Roman nails, from the villa that Lethbridge himself had excavated 24 years earlier.

Then the story took another twist. Gordon Fowler heard that a firm of solicitors paid Ford £20, in 1922 before he sold the land to farmer Rolfe, to dig for something in the field. Someone from overseas was privy to information that a secret treasure had been buried by a past occupant of Rolfe's house 'so many paces from the meadow gate'. They found nothing from their digging which took place 'near the road gate'.

Lethbridge realised there had been two different gateways when he spotted 'an old gate pintle' protruding from a tree-trunk some distance from the road. This single field had once been two. Apart from the tree, there were traces of a dividing hedge-line, that had been removed. Logically, he reasoned, no one would therefore risk digging a hole beside a public road when they owned an alternative spot that was safely out of sight.

Fowler and Lethbridge were sure that the solicitors had dug in the wrong place. Ford would have known about the second 'phantom' gateway, but had to wait two decades for the opportunity to explore in its vicinity, in a snowstorm. Fowler's researches came up with the name of Black Jack Seaber – not that he established a definitive spelling – who apparently figured in the book *Cheap Jack*

Zita by Sabine Baring-Gould (1834-1924) and was said to be a relative of the Cole Ambrose family of Stuntney, near Ely. They and he were great collectors of antiquities from rich Roman sites in Lincolnshire and Norfolk.

The archaeologists confirmed that this had indeed been the spot where something had been hidden. They found yellow-enamelled remains of a large trunk. It was most unlikely, however, that Seaber's magnificent finds had come from the little Roman house that was then concealed under an unploughed meadow.

Far more likely it had come from one of the many larger sites, upstream from Mildenhall, in the valley of the River Lark. Gordon Fowler interrogated Icklingham's parson and was introduced to someone with an old family Bible. A hand-written note, inserted circa 1860, recorded the discovery of "silver bells on Cavenham Heath".

These Cavenham 'bells' and the Mildenhall 'bowls' might be one and the same, Fowler postulated. Though only a little pocket of heathland it had documented form. Miss Nina Layard found a 'crown' of female diadems – made of silver head-bands – at the end of the Great War. Lethbridge himself had excavated there, uncovering 'two rifled Roman brick tombs', close to a later cemetery of more than 500 Anglo-Saxon cremation urns. All this had been crammed into a comparatively small area. After the ravages of modern agriculture all Colin Graham, Howard Pell and I could find was an expanse of arable nothingness. Lethbridge, however, had no doubt that with Fowler's help he had solved the puzzle:

'I am sure that this was the find-spot of the Mildenhall Treasure.'

Others thought the same. On 14 May 1991, *The New York Times* reported that the J. Paul Getty Museum in Malibu, California, had been 'eager to buy' a small Romano-British bronze figurine of a leopard for $600,000 in 1988. Dr Marion True, curator of antiquities, described it as 'one of the most important finds of the last 50 years' because of its 'extremely fine workmanship, advanced technology and iconographic and religious importance'. Distinguished by spots of inlaid silver, this was one of the so-called 'Icklingham Bronzes', comprising 15 pieces which had apparently been found with a metal-detector on wheat fields owned by John and Rosemary Browning, when they were ploughed during the winter. Its removal had been unauthorised and a law suit followed the leopard across the Atlantic, leading to the Getty Museum withdrawing from the transaction. The piece was eventually donated to the British Museum.

John Browning eloquently denounced the activities of 'nighthawks' at the Society of Antiquaries in London on 16 February 2009 and said that 'despite some 40 or 50 prosecutions, the theft of our common heritage has been going on for a generation'. Key evidence for Roman-period Christianity in Britain continued to be stolen with much being eventually dispersed and true find-spots being concealed or lost.

–7–
National Trust Reform

Chris Rundle, the environment reporter for the *Western Daily Press* who followed my adventures on Steep Holm, was the first to realise the news value of having me appointed to the 52-strong ruling council of the National Trust. Guy Somerset from Minehead, who I replaced as chairman of the Open Spaces Society, had stood down and I took his place in 1990. My question at the trust's Queen Anne's Gate headquarters about the demolition of an eighteenth-century stable block at Montacute House received a dismissive reply. Those sort of issues were not to be discussed. So the headline to Chris Rundle's story on 5 July 1990 caused dismay ('Trust mansion hit by vandalism row'). I also asked about the policy of hunting wildlife on trust land. 'We hear', *The Visitor* magazine reported, in August 1990:

> *'That the mouth of Wincanton writer Rodney Legg is still causing pain to others. That Mr Legg is the new appointee to the council of the National Trust and immediately after a long and heated debate on the licensing of hunting across trust land, the chairman, Dame Jennifer Jenkins, strode over to him and announced, "Our meetings are never lengthy, contentious or confrontational!".*

That mouth was to cause the wife of politician Roy Jenkins more grief over the next couple of months. It soon caused me to be 'spread all over the national media' on the eve of the trust's annual general meeting. National Trust spokesmen scurried around the country for a fortnight as they reacted to a barrage of criticism It was also hard work for me, as David Wilson wrote in the Bournemouth *Evening Echo* on 7 November 1990:

> *'Rodney Legg simply buzzes with energy. Just interviewing him took a lot of rapid walking as he rushed around packing up his car for yet another spot on television, fighting the good fight.'*

It was the most sustained media attention the trust had received since 1982 when word slipped out that an £80 million bomb-proof underground bunker had been secretly built beneath trust-owned land at Bradenham, near High Wycombe. It was currently acting as the command and control headquarters for Operation Granby in the Persian Gulf. 'Should the military ever relinquish Bradenham', editor Pat Dunion mused in *The Visitor:*

'... the National Trust might want to relocate there from Queen Anne's Gate; it must be just about Legg-proof.'

Paul Brown, among others, reported the schism in the *Guardian* on 23 October 1990 ('National Trust accused of betraying access ideals') across the top of the second page:

'A damning indictment of the National Trust for illegally blocking public footpaths, enclosing common land, and keeping secret its ownership of prestigious properties, including the home of Thomas Hardy, was made last night by Rodney Legg, chairman of the Open Spaces Society. Mr Legg, a National Trust council member, said the organisation fell short of its founders' ideals as a landowner. He added that the Ministry of Defence was often a better guardian of the natural landscape.'

The paper's cartoonist, David Austin, had a couple looking up at an 'NT' sign:

'I think it stands for "No Trespassing".'

The leader column in the *Independent* suggested that the National Trust should be split up. 'National Trust rejects an open and shut case' was the headline across the front of the *The Times*. 'When did the trust last make the front page of *The Times*?' Open Spaces Society secretary Kate Ashbrook asked, when trust public relations supremo Warren Davis wanted us to refund the £345 cost of booking a lecture room for me, which the National Trust had paid. That made it into *The Times* 'Diary' column. 'Mr Legg remembered his media opportunity rather than his manners', Colin Amery commented, in the *Financial Times*. The journal *Rural Socialism* summed up various 'Untrustworthy' accusations:

'Even more serious charges were brought by Rodney Legg, chairman of the Open Spaces Society [who] *pointed to the closure of some of the trust's most authentic properties; to the purchase of land for investment rather than conservation, resulting in intensive farming and landscape damage; to the illegal fencing of common land and the blockage of public rights of way. "From being an egalitarian access organisation promoting the public good," he said, "the trust has become an elitist club of art connoisseurs."*

'These charges have all the more force coming from an officer of the Open Spaces Society. Not only does Rodney Legg sit on the NT council as the society's nominee, but it was the OSS itself that founded National Trust for the purpose of "accepting, holding and purchasing open spaces for the people in town and city". There was nothing in this remit about stately homes.'

'Blistering' was the *Daily Telegraph*'s word for a lecture I delivered on 'Common Roots' in the Great Hall of the Royal Society of Arts on 22 October 1990. It marked the 125th anniversary of the Open Spaces Society, Britain's oldest

Max Gate, Dorchester, in Thomas Hardy's day – opening it to the public was Rodney Legg's campaign for a quarter of a century

'Nothing matters' – T. E. Lawrence's Greek motto above the door to Clouds Hill – with Rodney Legg photographed by Debbie Moore

national conservation body. I reminded the trust's hierarchy that my predecessors had founded the National Trust. It was now burdened 'by an archaic, undemocratic structure'. I called for a return to the trust's original 1895 ideals.

I attacked the trust for hiding its ownership of Max Gate in Dorchester, the home that Thomas Hardy built in 1885 and lived in to his death in 1928. Hardy's sister Kate – whose will I had obtained – left it to the National Trust in 1940 to be 'retained in its present condition as far as possible' but the trust had never opened it to the public. Hardy's study had been stripped out and put into Dorset County Museum in Dorchester. Items such as the tombstone of Hardy's dog Wessex (which bit John Galsworthy) and a prehistoric standing stone, were in the garden, unseen by the public.

It remained, however, a place of pilgrimage for Hardy's disciples, particularly as he was the only major novelist who designed and built the house where he wrote his principal works. Though scholars had been given access by prior arrangement, ordinary visitors were not welcome, and most only glimpsed a brick wall and canopy of dark trees. Max Gate did not appear in the publication *Properties of the National Trust* and trust's photographic archivist at Queen Anne's told me it was 'unknown' to charity's computer.

When it came to properties that did appear in listings and the annual *Handbook* I claimed that many had no informal access beyond their ha-ha, into parkland and the wider estates. Often they were managed by land-agents inherited from the last private owners who had '500 years experience in keeping the public out'.

Even public paths, where they did exist, were blocked on a number of properties. I took the media to see offending barbed wire across the Stourhead Estate in Wiltshire, made a television foray into the Peak District, and then stumbled into Hidcote Gardens in Gloucestershire where Open Spaces Society objections had led to a public inquiry. Seeking out path problems conveniently revealed that there was then no access to landscape features such as St Peter's Pump and Zeals Knoll in Wiltshire.

I complained that much of the Stonehenge downland, acquired as chalk grassland, was still being ploughed and that thousands of acres of farmland across the country had been acquired 'not for public enjoyment but for intensive agriculture':

'The trust owns 400 square miles of boring farmland which it should allow to revert to semi-wooded landscape shared by people and wildlife. That would start to balance the absurdity of the best-preserved Wiltshire downland being not the trust's land at Stonehenge and Avebury but the military ecology of the artillery ranges on Salisbury Plain.

'Since the 1930s, however, it has concentrated instead on conservation of the gentry. The trust has evolved into a major safety net for preventing the decline and fall of the English country home. In doing so it has saved an important element of the leisured landscape of the privileged from extinction. From being an egalitarian access organisation promoting the public good, the trust has become an elitist club of art connoisseurs, and defensive in the protection of a prize collection of dinosaurs.'

The story resumed the following weekend with half a page by Charles Oulton in the broadsheet *Independent on Sunday* ('Forbidden follies that provoked a public row') on 28 October. I had taken him around the Stourhead Estate to point out problems on the ground:

'Finding out anything about the National Trust is a bit like penetrating MI5, and criticising them is like criticising God or the Queen. One member of our society has resigned because of my remarks but I don't regret them. Something at last may now get done.'

Gillian Darley gave me a third of a page in the *Observer* ('It's open season on the Trust') likening it to 'Beatrix Potter's tale of Squirrel Nutkin and Mr Brown'. Catherine Bennett featured the continuing dispute in the *Guardian* of 10 November. She approached trust luminary and mastermind of country house acquisitions, James Lees-Milne, for his opinion on the problems the trust were experiencing with Rodney Legg:

'Is that that maddening man? That man is a perfect pest. I don't know why he got appointed. He's an awful fellow and he's making things awful for everybody, he's really a fiend of a man.'

Lees-Milne saw me as a latter-day Teagle, who called on him on 9 February 1944 (dates were daily currency for Lees-Milne who now lived from his diaries) as a devout young naturalist who attempted to distract him from his mission to save the English country house in order to consider acquiring some cherished piece of threatened ground. That, he argued, would be in line with the original objectives of the trust's founders. As for Max Gate, at the heart of the current debate, playwright George Bernard Shaw recommended 'Pull it down' and Lees-Milne advised the Historic Buildings Committee 'to sell it', Bennett wrote:

'The committee didn't sell Max Gate. But neither did they open it to the public. Now, 50 years later, this fact has been discovered and publicised by a man called Rodney Legg, a vegetarian, madly keen on nature. Rodney Legg is warden of a bird sanctuary, expert on ancient Dorset and furiously concerned with unlocked gates. He is not, one feels sure, a man to wipe his nose on the back of his hand, but in other ways, at least in the way he is seen by the trust, Rodney Legg is a Teagle . . . Legg's crime, perhaps unique in the 95-year history of the National Trust, was to cause a scene.'

After the trust's annual general meeting in November I exposed the secret use of 40,000 'blank' proxy votes. These had been given to the chairman, Dame Jennifer Jenkins, who used them to beat attempts to ban hunting on trust land. Describing this as 'the handbag vote' – an allusion to Mrs Thatcher which displeased Dame Jennifer – I said it broke with convention to use such discretionary proxies to reverse a decision instead of reinforce it. *The Sunday Times* quoted me on 23 December 1990:

'It is a scandal that she did not tell us the size of her votes, because the council has a responsibility to take a decision based on full information.'

Dame Jennifer, who was standing down at the end of the year, asked top-people's lawyer Lord Arnold Goodman about the prospects for a libel action. The advice must have been cautionary as no writ was forthcoming. Stronger reactions came from Auberon Waugh. Forgetting that he had once bought me a gin and tonic in a train, he satirised me under the heading 'Square leg' in his *Daily Telegraph* column on 29 December:

'Hand the National Trust over to these unpleasant, wrong headed fanatics and there will be very little left to celebrate in Britain. We are approaching one of those rare moments when every citizen must say "So far and no further".'

My intervention in the hunting debate – mainly to criticise the undemocratic nature of the trust's decision-making procedures 'in a rash of newspaper articles' – was analysed by *The Great Outdoors* in May 1991. It went on to highlight shortcomings in the trust's regional old boy network of largely self-appointed committees. I had been ostracised from fellow council members though one was quoted having phoned me after a meeting:

'Do you know who I am? I did feel for you today. You took a real hammering and if I had gone through the same I would say sod the trust, but you must carry on, don't give up, there are several of us who agree with you, but we can't come out and say it.'

Ed Douglas rounded off his feature by quoting David Beskine of the Ramblers' Association:

'If it wasn't Rodney Legg it would be someone else later. The trust doesn't like him because he doesn't play the game. They can't take the wind of democracy. They cannot take dissent. So they don't like Rodney Legg. Well that's tough.'

Reading some of the cuttings for the first time, two decades later, can produce some surprises. My Wimborne friend Pip – the late Phillipa Oakes-Ash – always gave me credit for saving the Vine Inn at Pamphill, by embarrassing the trust into not disposing of this Bankes Estate 'alienable' asset. She saw contemporary trust documents and my responses each week as they happened. What I meant to say, however, was rather garbled by Ian McKay in a feature in the *Antique Collector* in the summer of 1991:

'On one side there is the resistance to any kind of commercial venture, as voiced by Legg over the trust's running of the Vine public house in Dorset. It came to the trust as part of an estate and is still run as a pub – Legg would prefer that they sold the pub and put the money towards 12,000 acres of Welsh common land.'

My Dorset credentials and drinking propensities ruled out the former option but if such a reaction was to block the latter opportunity then I would be in a dilemma. I was presented with a similar choice on Channel 4 News in recent times and admitted that whilst I approved the purchase of Seaton Delaval Hall as Sir John Vanbrugh's great Northumbrian masterpiece, it would be a totally different matter if the alternative was the acquisition of another mile or two of nearby Hadrian's Wall.

In March 1991 I supported efforts of Commander Tom Foden to beat a ban on the *Balmoral* pleasure steamer landing on Lundy Island which the Landmark Trust manages for the National Trust. The *Western Mail* quoted me:

'This is another case of elitist access only to properties that are supposedly managed on behalf of us all. Ironically, the **Balmoral** *generally carried National Trust members and other elements of the middle classes rather than the bucket-*

and-spade brigade. The National Trust seems to have forgotten its roots.'

On 19 June 1991 the Bournemouth *Evening Echo* reported me giving the trust a pat on the back ('Trust work praised by arch-critic') for restoring chalk downland on Ballard Down, taking Studland Heath out of agriculture, and providing paths near Worth Matravers.

'I've stopped kicking what has become an open door,' Mr Legg added.

That was premature. On 4 November 1991, Toby Moore described me in the *Daily Telegraph* as the sole council member of the National Trust publicly opposed to hunting, having accused its new chairman, Lord Chorley, of using his discretionary proxy votes to ensure that a slate of anti-hunt campaigners was not elected to join us:

'It's like the bad old days of trades union block votes. Whereas there might be a case for using proxies to implement trust policy or block dotty ideas, it is against natural justice to use them to choose between personalities.'

Determined not to become a single-issue fanatic, I questioned the wisdom of the trust accepting sponsorship from a commercial peat-digging company, as the *Sunday Telegraph* reported on 17 November 1991:

'If Fisons are trying to get a green image, they should just stop peat digging.'

Such potentially controversial decisions should have been put before the trust's council but in practice this seldom happened. Following the trust council's first-ever official visit to our Northern Ireland properties, in July 1992, I wrote a feature for *The Countryman* which editor Christopher Hall entitled 'An Orange shade of green'. The text seems balanced and harmless in retrospect, as indeed Roger Chorley reassured me at the time – 'if you had written it about Northumberland'. Ireland, however, was an ultra-senstitive place. No one acknowledged that there was something going on in the province that approached civil war. Making this comment was asking for trouble:

'Inevitably, the trust is seen by some as an arm of the British establishment, floating on public grants. Though it makes a point of being neutral, the fact was that we had police surveillance following us discreetly as protection from unmentioned forces, and the administration has Scots-Irish names in abundance. They always seemed to know the affiliation, origins and religion (not that any was ever mentioned) of everyone we met. Somehow there is an identification coding that is intuitive to all in this split community. They took it for granted that at Mount Stewart, admiring the begonia-bed cut into the gravel, we were standing beside a huge floral representation of the Red Hand – the badge of Ulster.'

National Trust Director-General Angus Stirling
photographed Rodney Legg with a dinosuar at Mount
Stewart, Northern Ireland, in 1992

Other unwelcome observations included the
failure to determine how many 'from the other side
of the community' were on the trust's regional
committee. The answer was 'maybe two' out of 14,
not that we met either of them, though that was
hardly surprising given that we never left County
Down. There might have been a tourist industry at
the time, but we were told it was a bluff, and
regional chairman Professor Ronnie Buchanan added that there was no tradition
of public paths in the province. If there were ordinary holiday-makers, they
would be back-packing at minimal expense through Antrim, to the coastal
spectaculars of the Giant's Causeway and the Donegal corner of the Republic:

*'We, the National Trust, have the best scenery of the United Kingdom's six
counties of Ulster, provide the only open space, act as the single conservation
organisation for the province, and yet the general population regards us as
irrelevant. That was the message I got. All the properties we saw were
undervisited. There are plenty of buses and Rowallane is only 20 minutes out
of Belfast, with banks of rhododendron and azalea, but fewer than 50 of us
from a coach overran the place and intimidated the three real visitors. Here
and elsewhere the layout of drives and parking belong to the days of the horse
and cart; clearly the 53-seater coach will have to be an innovation of Ulster's
twenty-first century.'*

Back home I was told to 'beware of the long hand of Ulster'. The official
backlash came from regional director Ian McQuiston: With 'anger and deeply-
felt hurt' he accused me of 'mere assertion' by making 'snide, inaccurate
generalisations' and 'cheap shots'. As 'fellow citizens of the United Kingdom,
many of us take great exception to being referred to as "natives" as if he had
stumbled on some undiscovered tribe' (but imagine the rage if I had called them
'settlers'). This was answered by the journal's editor:

*'If Mr Legg wants to comment on the position of the trust in Ulster in
relation to the social, political and civil problems to which the province is
subject, then it seems to me he has every right to do so. These things are of
interest to us on this side of the water. Of course, had I wanted a purely
descriptive piece about the work of the trust in Northern Ireland, I could have
sought one – and it would probably have been the usual dull reading that these
thing make. I preferred to use Mr Legg's certainly personal but livelier piece.'*

Judging from his letters, however, an Ian McQuiston article would be anything but dull. To another complainant, cancelling his subscription to the journal, Chris Hall pointed out that I was 'a member of the trust's council, not its public relations officer'. Personally, I had greatly enjoyed the trip, and Ian Mcquiston's company, and the offending feature was an attempt at deploying my residual talents as a journalist, rather than mischief-making.

Meanwhile I was now working with Wessex regional director David Bett to open more Wiltshire and Dorset paths, as I confirmed in the journal *Landscape Design:*

> *'These difficulties are being sorted out by the trust with what has become commendable alacrity and I am pleased to be co-operating with them to find a solution to more intractable dilemmas on the extensive Golden Cap estate in west Dorset where landform geology has complicated the position with a series of landslips. Two walkers are said to have drowned whilst attempting to follow the Pathfinder map. That shows the imperative of having paths on the map coinciding with the reality on the ground and David Bett and I are working together towards that end.'*

I retrospect, I wish I had exposed the inside story of the debacle that prevented us saving beautiful early-Tudor Pitchford Hall in Shropshire. It turned into pure cock-up after the trust asked the Treasury for £10 million to buy a property and its contents that were on the market for £1.8 million. We had lost touch with reality – the black-timbered house subsequently sold for £750,000. 'No more Pitchfords!' the Prince of Wales told the hierarchy, as I recalled when we intervened sensibly and successfully to save Tyntesfield (Victorian) and Seaton Delaval (Baroque).

There were other distractions at the time, ranging from fencing of common land in the Quantock Hills, and stag-hunting there and on Exmoor, to Hindhead Common, where I joined the trust's spokesmen in expressing outrage at:

> *'. . . this vicious plan to hack a road through the best vestiges of virgin heathland in south-east England'.*

I was also successfully fighting a road scheme in Dorset where the Cranborne Chase escarpment was threatened by a relief road at Melbury Abbas. I supported 'the grandees', inspired and led by Michael Pitt-Rivers against 'the philistines' and 'retired newcomers' (the order of battle described by Patrick Wright in *Guardian Weekend* on 12 June 1993). I led the opposition to a 'blue route' that would have taken the road on a detour deep into the downlands in order to avoid Melbury Abbas village. This compromise had been backed by the National Trust which did not want to be 'blindly obstructive':

> *'The hell with that – we represent the interests of the scenery, the sheep, and the wildlife rather than cosy cottagers.'*

That did not go down too well with the inhabitants or the *Western Gazette* ('Demolish homes says Trust stalwart') but I managed to shame the trust into opposing both routes. In west Dorset I called for the proposed Chideock-Morcombelake by-pass to be turned into a 'scenic slow road'. Neither road scheme proceeded.

Meanwhile my campaign to open Thomas Hardy's Max Gate home received fresh impetus from the news that its tenants, Bill and Vera Jesty, planned to depart. Their rent went towards the upkeep of Hardy's birthplace on the opposite bank of the River Frome, to which the trust provided public access, but I made the case in the *Western Daily Press* on 28 July 1993 that Max Gate should no longer be a 'secret property' shown only to scholars:

> *'Max Gate itself is the far more interesting of the two, because Hardy built it and wrote most of his major works there. There are Hardy societies all over the world now and the house has become a real magnet for them. But we have had Hardy enthusiasts travelling from the USA and Japan to visit the house and not understanding when they haven't been allowed to see it, especially when they have been told it is owned by the trust. What the trust doesn't seem to appreciate is that it is of far more interest because Hardy built it and lived in it than some place where he just happened to be born.'*

The tenants left in November 1993 and the National Trust agreed to take the opportunity to share 'the ultimate Hardy shrine' with the novelist's admirers. There was another 'secret' property I continued to 'out' to the irritation of trust staff. An irate member had phoned me on one of the first mobile phones – the size of a brick – as he was intercepted on the cliff at Redend Point, above Studland Bay. Noises-off in the background were from a warden who knew nothing of the blockhouse which I had been publicising for its key role in preparations for the Normandy landings:

> *'He's saying no, I can't see it – "You can't see it because it doesn't exist"!'*

It would take another decade for Fort Henry to return to our story. My views on National Trust land sales were reported in the *Sunday Express Magazine* ('A matter of Trust') in January 1994:

> *'I can see why people would be upset about Britain being turned into a theme park. It will have a negative effect on trust-giving. The trust has become overstretched. There is obviously a diminishing potential for some of our properties and it is perhaps a pity that in some cases the trust ever took them on. I wish we hadn't gone as far as we have with acquiring properties which need high revenue to keep them intact.'*

Properties in difficulty included Belton House in the East Midlands (£500,000 conservation work), Sudbury Hall near Derby (£500,000 roof) and Hardwick Hall, between Nottingham and Sheffield (£3,000,000 restoration). Work at Kingston Lacy House, Dorset, was being funded by selling land around

Wimborne in Dorset, leading to new housing estates being perceived 'as National Trust developments':

'What is happening at Hardwick Hall is that the trust has been selling other properties on the estate – cottages, land and farms – in order to fund it. I think it is a shame that the trust decided to make these purchases in the first place. But now we have got this burden of lots of country houses with expensive upkeep, it is inevitable that places are becoming a burden on the general membership.'

I became nation-wide spokesman for the 20 villages in trust ownership, such as Pumpsaint in Dyfed where the Dolecothi Arms Hotel closed after Dolecothi Gold Mines were turned into a Roman-inspired tourist honeypot. Things like this would never have happened under the benign feudalism of the last squire, James Hills Johnes VC, hero of the siege of Delhi. Peter Dunn quoted me in the *Independent* ('Can we have our squire back?') on 15 February 1994:

'I'm not against local museums-cum-theme-parks as such, but we should be preserving this kind of Celtic fringe community without inflicting 20th-century overkill or cultural imperialism directed from London. When people like the villagers of Pumpsaint want to return to feudalism, it must show we're doing something wrong somewhere.'

With a book entitled *National Trust Centenary* I jumped the gun and marked the occasion a year early, in 1994, to claim two of its three founders – namely Miss Octavia Hill and Sir Robert Hunter – as my predecessors in the Commons Preservation Society which provided the trust with its first offices and is

Celebrating with the National Trust at Studland Manor after opening Fort Henry to the public, photographed by John Pitfield

now the Open Spaces Society. Describing trust membership as 'almost entirely white, aged and middle class', I called for a crusade 'to make the National Trust truly representative of the nation as a whole, rather than a clone of its membership, and trigger the enthusiasm of all categories and cultures that make up Britain's complex cosmopolitan mix'. I called for better and more public access, including adoption of a Swedish-style Allemansratt – freedom to roam – across trust-owned farmland and open country in general. My diverse themes were summarised by Fanny Charles with these extracts for her lively *Blackmore Vale Magazine:*

> *'The agricultural situation in the Lake District is becoming an economic farce and a landscape disaster. Not only do Lakeland sheep represent £35 a head in annual subsidy payments, but they are clearly reverting into feral animals. Stocking levels of the high commons have doubled in the past decade – to take advantage of subsidies – and conspicuous path erosion on the fells is now being largely caused by over-grazing and flock movements . . .*
>
> *'Many of these flocks now have no economic purpose, beyond being paper entries for the purpose of subsidy applications. They are no longer being shorn, dipped or tended in any way, they are not culled for meat, and neither are many of the lambs removed from the fells. If the climate were drier up there, then they would be creating a desert . . .*
>
> *'Not only are young people failing to join the trust in any numbers but neither are members of our considerable ethnic communities. It is as if they have no cultural tradition of outdoor pursuits or countryside recreation . . .*
>
> *'Octavia Hill would point out that there was no custom of countryside access for all classes of the host community until her day, when the railways liberated the people to venture into the hills on the single afternoon of the week that they were not working. Things have improved on that score but the National Trust is still only a fragile partnership between privilege and the people.'*

I was encouraged by Sir John Smith, a former Conservative MP who founded the Landmark Trust to plug a hole in the trust's facade, as he confirmed to Paula Weideger when she compiled her book *Gilding the Acorn*:

> *'What Sir John must mean is that he has a weakness for mavericks. Take for instance Rodney Legg. Legg represents the Open Spaces Society on the National Trust's ruling Council. He appears to be a cross between a feral man of the wild and an advertising whiz kid (the former image, perhaps, being an example of the latter gift). When Legg wants to criticise the trust for failing to keep some footpath open, or otherwise exercise proper vigilance about public access to its countryside properties, he manages to get thousands of words of press coverage. Noticing this, the trust asked Legg to serve as a member of his countryside access review committee, which he did. "They'd rather have me inside the tent pissing out; than outside pissing in." Legg*

wrote his own account of the trust's history as a countryside preservation body, which he published for its centenary. It is dedicated to Sir John Smith, "who brought me back into the fold".'

The reward was a day-out, along with John Pitfield as my partner, at the heart of the establishment for a Buckingham Palace garden party on 20 July 1995. I told the Queen that I regularly invoked her name. On being asked what I am doing on a path, usually whilst snipping my way across a stile with secateurs, I have a stock reply:

'Trying to proceed along the Queen's highway !'

The Queen was amused and said it reminded her of a television documentary, showing footage of the first Kenyan national parks, in her father's time. The natives were continuing to spear the wildlife, and in order to make them desist, officials declared that these were now the 'King's animals'. Her Majesty repeated the phrase 'Queen's highways' and I added that I would continue to defend them, but hoped that she would be spared any direct letter writing on the matter. From John Pitfield she learnt that his contribution to the environment was firing rockets into it. Then came the son, and I suggested that Prince Charles should create a new village green, as the focal point for his Poundbury estate at Dorchester.

At the time I was trying to thwart the trust's purchase of 800 acres of downland at the Devil's Dyke and adjoining Saddlescombe Farm from Brighton Borough Council. Evidence was produced that the land had been acquired 'in perpetuity' between 1885 and 1947 'for the use of the public for ever'. The *Estates Gazette* of 5 August 1995 reported my argument that this was 'an appalling example to other local authorities' who would be tempted to dump conservation-grade land on the National Trust and other charities, as indeed they have:

'It is both a precedent and an outrage. The fraud is that it will use new money to pay for old assets – money that could go to purchase land that is private and under threat from mismanagement and development. The National Trust must be dissuaded from playing this game. Saving the Devil's Dyke twice is the devil's work.'

The *BBC Wildlife Magazine* expanded on my quotes:

'This land was already in public ownership and protected in perpetuity, yet here is the National Trust paying for it all over again. This is all money that could be going to buying new land. The whole thing is totally immoral. We have already gone to the great British public once and got them to pay for things, and now we are going back and asking them to pay all over again.'

Instead I had been urging that the trust should celebrate its centenary by buying Land's End as an iconic addition to its Enterprise Neptune acquisitions.

the *Daily Telegraph* carried a letter from me calling it 'the ultimate superlative in coastal properties'. It came on the market when Standard Chartered Bank dismantled Peter de Savary's business empire. My vision was to turn the peninsula from an eyesore into a treasure by placing the car-park underground. the *Cornishman* quoted me on 22 February 1996:

'After all there's only one Land's End. One isn't being unduly xenophobic to fear that foreign or faceless ownership in the form of the next consortium of buyers could well turn tackiness into an environmental nightmare.'

On both scores I failed. The Devil's Dyke is trust-owned and Land's End is not. I also caused a fuss about the trust carrying out gorse-burning on Shute Shelve in the Mendip Hills, arguably for the benefit of the rare Dartford warbler, though Somerset ornithologist Tony Parsons agreed with me that they had probably been smoked out:

'The bird does not nest anywhere else in Somerset – and we do not have a lot of suitable habitats anywhere else. It relies on gorse for feeding off in the winter and if the gorse has gone the habitat has gone. There is no possibility of the bird surviving there. Whatever has happened there it is too late now, but we must prevent any lack of communication like this occurring again.'

A Dorset lost cause concerned the Dorset home of Lawrence of Arabia. A chalet bungalow opposite had been demolished and replaced by a suburban-style house for the trust's warden. Then most of the rhododendrons planted by Lawrence, to ensure his privacy, were cut down. *The Guardian* of 14 June 1997 reported my complaints that this was:

'. . . a violation of the spirit of the place. It has destroyed the character of Clouds Hill as T. E. Lawrence knew it.'

I provided a list of trust disposals and speculative development projects for *The Sunday Times* of 3 August 1997 ('National Trust sells properties to developers'). It was 'selling the family silver', I declared:

'This is asset-stripping. Something has gone wrong with the trust's philosophy. You have got to keep faith with past benefactors to encourage new ones. We are going to regret this.'

Spokeswoman Caroline Audemars replied that financial advisers thought returns from those investments were much lower than for money invested in stocks and shares, 'so we have been selling more of it off'.

Stag-hunting remained the big controversy and I kept up the flow of inside news, such as in the *Guardian* ('Trust chiefs uphold ban against deer hunting') and *Daily Telegraph* ('Huntsmen fight on after National trust backs deer ban') on 3 October

1997. My 'gloves off' contribution, to John Vidal in the *Guardian* of 7 November 1997, concerned a pro-hunting group calling itself FONT (Friends Of the National Trust) that was standing for election to council:

'They should have called themselves FRONT, Fascists Ratting On the National Trust . . . It's a very dangerous, disguised take-over bid. The eight have put themselves forward as ordinary country-loving folk but their real agenda is different. If elected, this group could cause real trouble.'

Remarkably, given my firebrand reputation as 'a convincing imitation of a loose cannon' (John Newth in *Dorset Life*), one of my terms as a trust council member – from 1998 to 2001 – was the result of election by the membership, but I then reverted to being an appointee of the Open Spaces Society. I continued to condemn a proxy voting system that left the chairman with thousands of blank votes to apply at will. By 2001 this had been compounded by the recommendations of an appointments committee – which I dubbed the 'Star Chamber' – that placed asterisks beside a slate of chosen names. It is difficult to sex-up elections and governance for the national press but Colette Jackson of the *Western Gazette* managed to make it interesting to the home audience on 30 August 2001 ('National Trust rejects vote-rigging claims') and let me put my case:

'The system that they have gone for is using the old Labour Party asterisk system. It is basically control freakery. It is suggesting to members how they should vote . . . The establishment may regard me as subversive but fellow members of the council have called me the conscience of the trust.'

Our chairman at this time, Charles Nunneley, maintained the tradition of coming to an unspoken consensus rather than taking votes at meetings, but someone suggested we should start acting like other organisations, on 24 January 2002. I agreed and said:

'When I used to vote I was the only one who did so but I still lost the vote. We should at least have a vote now on whether or not to have voting.'

It was not put to the vote. Neither was the practice of using asterisks to indicate recommended voting at annual general meetings, despite Neil Edwards – who was on the 'Star Chamber' – saying he had changed his mind about it, because it gave the trust 'absolute power'. Neil recommended its abandonment. Most of the comments were against the practice but again the status quo was maintained. I protested that the spirit of the meeting was being ignored and asked for my vote against to be recorded. 'With Mr Legg dissenting', the chairman said. No one else ever joined me even at moments like that.

We endorsed a Charity Commission requirement that we had agreed to the use of part of our capital growth as income. This was quite a fundamental investment move, so it was asked whether they required a vote, but again there was none. The accountant explained a graph showing how capital growth enabled the release of income while still protecting the overall appreciation of investments. The graph, I pointed out, was out of synchronisation with its dates, because these showed the high point of shares continuing for three years after the Wall Street Crash. Nunneley beamed:

'As I noticed as well but presentations by accountants are always like that.'

Charles was coming to the end of his term and a special appointments committee was created. The chairman agreed to stay until they found a suitable replacement, which gave me the best laugh of the meeting, for a comment involving a former Director-General of the BBC:

'If we delay, will Lord Birt be available?'

My Dorset campaigning success of 2002 was the opening to the public of the monolithic concrete Fort Henry observation post from where Winston Churchill and Allied top-brass, joined by King George VI on 18 April 1944, watched live-firing rehearsals for the Normandy landings. Just about 100 feet in length, with walls and roof three-feet thick, it stands on the seaward side of the Manor House Hotel at Redend Point, overlooking Studland Bay. The trust hosted the re-opening in style and we were led by actor Graham Gadd as our cigar-smoking Churchill look-alike on the 58th anniversary of Exercise Smash, plus the American 1st Infantry Division Living History Company, and real-life 87-year-old Bill Chutter from Dorchester who was there at the time with the 1st Battalion of the Dorsetshire Regiment. Celia Mead, from the trust's Wessex office, masterminded the project and its opening.

Having often complained that the trust was 'London-centric' I welcomed the chance to see plans for a new headquarters, in light-looking architecture behind a wall of glass and grey engineering bricks, on the site of Churchward's engineering works at Swindon in March 2003. I paid a compliment to the plan and rejected the notion that it should be 'greened' by rows of trees:

'It is the site of locomotive yards. If you want to see bright greens they are everywhere in the next building – the Steam Museum – in the liveries of great railway engines like **Caerphilly Castle.**'

What I did not like about governance changes, Peter Hetherington reported in the *Guardian* on 6 September 2003 ('Bourgeois image haunts National Trust') was that City grandee Lord Blakenham had steered us from being a ruling council into an almost powerless body that appointed a board of trustees to make all the decisions:

'The whole thing is controlled as if it were National Trust PLC, rather than a charity.'

The changes were pushed through by Ms Fiona Reynolds (now Dame Fiona) as our reformist Director-General and the new chairman, financier and landowner Sir William Proby. 'Campaigning' made its debut on the trust's agenda. Once upon a time we used to be told it was 'a non-Trust word'. Genetically modified trials on our land needed approval if they were for experimentation rather than agricultural purposes. I stressed that if any such permission was being considered, the issue should be brought to us for reappraisal, because it was supposed to be a long-standing custom that controversial matters were up to the council to determine. Not that anyone asked what we thought about the shooting of the ruddy duck in Tatton Park, Cheshire. Young males were said to be flying off to the Mediterranean on holiday and copulating with their Spanish cousins. There was something, however, that ornithologists were not telling us:

'It's all Peter Scott's fault because he brought them across from America to enliven things at Slimbridge.'

'Pink weddings' were discussed on 18 March 2004 when we were asked to approve a minute from the previous meeting:

'It reaffirmed its policy of non-discrimination but agreed that the trust should not be involved in any promotional activity through the media or any other channel to encourage the use of trust properties for these ceremonies.'

I said this put a homophobic gloss on what had been decided and asked for assurances that bookings for such ceremonies were still being accepted. My understanding that 'we may enable but don't encourage' was confirmed as the policy. It was a lifestyle from which Robin Page dissented, saying that ordinary members of the trust and the clientele at the Dog and Duck were outraged. He picked on my 'politically correct' words to the effect that things which were legal were allowable on trust land, saying he could think of activities that we would shy away from, and instanced the present case. I intervened to get a laugh:

'Robin, it's not compulsory!'

He might have capped that with the word 'Yet' but fortunately he didn't and we moved on to next business.

In 2007, though still a council member of the trust, I was resigned to no longer being a trustee. The century-old exercise in representative democracy, with 26 elected members and a similar number of appointees from appropriate bodies, ended as our powers passed to an inner cabinet of super-trustees. For several years I had been the single vote against the revisionist process.

Like turkeys, the rest voted for Christmas, with a Parliamentary scheme which was approved on 20 March 2005 and came into effect a couple of years later. To me, lawyers and accountants brought about the disabling of the old trust. Grey men in suits manipulated the good and the great as those who presumed to know the law joined with others whose grasp on two-plus-two landed us in an economic black hole. What had become a £75 million deficit in our employee pension fund was swallowing £5 million from current revenue every year. It threatened the scourge of redundancy as staffing levels were reduced to the core 5,000.

A staff survey showed that only 15 per cent 'feel that senior managers are in touch with what is happening on the ground'. That 15 per cent, I suggested, probably represented the senior managers themselves. Often, after they leave or retire, disillusioned employees talk of disconnection and duplication throughout the trust. 'Frustrating and senseless', one told me in Devon, after moving back to the private sector as a land agent. Tenants were also showing unease. Rent arrears rose to £4.5 million

I questioned our land management philosophy. Where the Forestry Commission had taken the plunge and dedicated its freehold woodlands as open country under the provisions of the Countryside and Rights of Way Act, the National Trust feared to tread. The trust, second in size in terms of acreage, refused to follow the example which commission chairman Lord Clark put into effect throughout the national woodlands.

Even where the National Trust has areas which are subject to a right to roam, such as on Snowdon's southern slopes, there are often few stiles or other access points. Trust wisdom is that people might otherwise stray, and need rescuing, with the emphasis in Snowdonia being put on paths up the iconic mountain which cost £800,000. Reluctant to re-open old quarries, which it owns, or to disturb scree-slopes, the trust shipped stone steps from China for the project. These were then lowered by helicopter. I mused that in millennia to come, geology students may puzzle over the global potential for glacial drift.

Though I welcomed a widening of the criteria and scope for trust acquisitions, I was disappointed that despite record sums from appeals and legacies, the scale of purchases had slumped to the lowest level in decades. Having acted as a safety net, during their threatened period, for the English country house and their owner's lifestyles, we were now paying the price.

Sir William Proby correctly pointed out that our property portfolio is a liability rather than an asset. The same applies to conserving the collection of cultural artefacts. Land and chattels are worth billions but cannot be sold. They have to be maintained in the trust's slogan 'for ever, for everyone' at ever-increasing expense to ourselves and our successors. To their credit, Proby and Reynolds were soon to steer us through to the successful acquisition of Sir John Vanbrugh's palatial Seaton Delaval Hall in sight of the coast near Blyth, Northumberland. Its grand all-stone stables are a temple to the horse. I despaired that instead of bringing them back we might turn them into yet another tea-room (just as Tudor walled gardens used to be regarded as ideal for the car-park).

In January 2007, the standing of my Open Spaces Society as a nominating body to the National Trust council was under serious threat. An internal appointments committee proposed our deletion. The day was saved, Fiona Reynolds told society secretary Kate Ashbrook, by an emotional speech without notes in which I spelt out how we had been responsible for the parentage of the National Trust. Peter Nixon, as boss of conservation work, intervened to agree and went on to explain how we also provided the trust's first office, and continued to provide him with invaluable expertise and support on common land dilemmas.

In the event it was the Linnean Society and quango concerned with the national curriculum that found themselves dropped. I was lucky that the Royal Society for the Protection of Birds declined to put itself forward. The problem is that inclusion eventually depends upon a vote of the members and they will tend to go for known bodies – such as the RSPB – rather than something more esoteric. The council voted 'overwhelmingly' (chairman Proby's word) to reinstate the Open Spaces Society on the recommended list. Fiona Reynolds commented:

'That was Rodney's finest hour.'

At times I despaired of explaining what the society represented. As governance calls for an accelerated turnover of council members, several have no idea of the trust's history, though ignorance has a long pedigree, as was shown by the lady who asked at my first meeting:

'Isn't the National Trust rather on the fringes for you in the allotments movement?'

Paradoxically, the trust is now providing land for allotments. The issue then went to the membership where, it turned out, we were still trusted. Open Spaces Society came ninth (with 28,272 votes) in the list of 26 nominating bodies. Top was the Royal Horticultural Society (29,828 votes) and our vote narrowly beat that for the Ramblers' Association (tenth with 28,026 votes). The eight bodies that were nominated though not recommended, by an internal trust committee, all failed to be elected. Their support ranged from a respectable 9,297 (for English Heritage) to a derisory 1,221 (Qualifications and Curriculum Authority). In fairness to both winners and losers it should be noted that the level of participation was pathetic for an electorate of 3.5 million.

All we now seemed to discuss was our own governance though I still tried to draw attention to real issues. In January 2006 I found a fascinating aside on risks and responsibilities that was tucked away in a report. It concerned the number of us (an estimated 40 per cent of the population) who pass water through National Trust properties (in my case the River Stour). My observation was that a high percentage of the water we use – I never drink it – comes from rainfall on trust land.

There had been a recent row about communications and confidentiality. As a result we were circulated with former Director-General Angus Stirling's memorandum on collective responsibility, from 1991, which was a reaction and response to revelations by me. My retaliation, then and now, was:

'Firstly I am only collectively responsible for decisions in which I participated. In those days we only rubber-stamped things that others had already decided

89

for us. Secondly, and this was agreed at the time, Dame Jennifer Jenkins conceded that I could register my dissent on ethical grounds to any offensive decision. Four stick in mind – killing deer on National Trust land, gassing badgers on our land, shooting ruddy duck on our land, and now subsidising farmers to sponge off our land.'

On the other hand I defended our decision on farm rationalisations in Beatrix Potter country, at the annual general meeting in Liverpool and in a letter to *The Times* on 26 November 2005. Mrs Heelis, as the trust knew her, was a formidably pragmatic lady who ruled her Lake District farms utterly dispassionately. I urged the trust's new board of trustees to resist attempts at turning us into the 'National Farmers Preservation Society'. In particular I opposed efforts by landowner Henry Keswick and countryman Robin Page to resist changes which were turning five hill farms into four:

'I can't see what all the fuss is about. The farm buildings are still there. The fields are still there. The hedges are still there. The walls are still there. The sheep are still there.

'That's all the visitors and trust members see. The rest is a redistribution of percentages in bank accounts between five struggling farm businesses which are now a notch more viable as four struggling farm businesses. All business is a struggle but that is no reason for saying that the trust as an environmental charity should start subsidising its farmers. Some want to see us doing just that. Instead of collecting rent we will be paying them to live in the Lake District.'

I argued that because trust ownership is in perpetuity it has to adapt to change as patterns of farming and vegetation ebb and flow across the upland slopes as they have done for centuries. One day it will be glaciers that return.

Down on the coast I took issue with a statement that the long-running Neptune campaign to save Britain's coastline needed a 'new rallying call'. It remains a battle being fought rather than a war that has been won. In places it has worsened the conservation situation by attracting the new rich who have flocked to live in the places we have saved:

'We need to buy the future which lies in the fields behind the shore. Otherwise we become squeezed, literally, as the barrier between people and the sea – and the previously comfortable existence of those drawn to life on the coast. We have moved on from being a safeguard and are now seen as part of the problem rather than the solution. Strategic thinking means capturing minds for the wider vision. We need to secure not just the place but its setting.'

I suggested as slogans 'New Neptune' and 'Securing the Setting'. Another phrase might be 'Linking Landscapes' which was a refinement of a 'Living Landscapes' idea that had started the debate. I had been trying to encourage much-needed physical linkage between conurbations and the countryside. The intervention was mis-understood, however, as being a call for efforts against coastal erosion.

My last stand against replacement of our ruling council as a fiduciary body by a new all-powerful board of trustees centred on what seemed to be an Ulster loophole. It was spotted by Bernard Selwyn of the Open Spaces Society who argued that a lapse in amending the National Trust Acts had left our council in charge of Trust properties in Northern Ireland. Matters came to a head at a rather disputatious meeting with Parliamentary draftsmen Winckworth Sherwood at offices in Great Peter Street, Westminster, on 18 January 2007 (the day of the Great Gale). Incidentally their founder, Stephen Winckworth, was a member of the general committee of our Commons Preservation Society in 1883.

It was depressing as Bernard's points were largely ignored and my only positive contribution was to be there. Otherwise, I fear, Stephen Wiggs would have rejected Bernard's standing on the matter. He questioned whether life membership of the trust, from a London address, was sufficient. I intervened to claim higher-level status, as Open Spaces Society chairman, and therefore the direct descendant representing the organisation that was pre-eminent in the founding of the trust, having provided all nine of the signatories in its original articles of association, plus its first offices and secretary. This was from 1894 through to the time when it bought its first Irish property (a castle in what is now the Irish Republic), which was before the first National Trust Act, and that as a member of National Trust council since 1990 I was a trustee for this and the other (Northern) Ireland properties. Stephen Wiggs said they no longer owned the castle in question. I answered that the trust had never relinquished the freehold, but let it on what amounted to a perpetual lease. Bernard confidently told the lawyers:

'I can read an Act of Parliament and this one does not cover more than the law of property. It does not cover membership – which remains set at ten shillings for 1907 – or bye-laws or restrictive covenants. The trust's 1971 Act does have powers relating to such things but Northern Ireland is specifically excluded from it. Northern Ireland special provisions, including the 1946 Act, are entirely omitted from the trust's own governance handbook.'

The parliamentary agent and the trust said they were aware of possible shortcomings but had been reassured by a highly-respected constitutional QC that they would not arise in practice. This opinion would have to be taken at face value as they would not part with copies of such advice. The matter had been properly put before the trust's annual general meeting and ratified in the form of a resolution, in 2006. If there was a need for further powers, they doubted these would be of much significance, and could await incorporation into a National Trust Bill in the distant future. They would give us a letter to this effect. All Bernard could do in reply was to diplomatically suggest that all this amounted to shoddy drafting:

'*Private legislation intended to be effective in separate parts of the United Kingdom should not be misleading. It should not require a QC to explain the meaning. Its lack of transparency must be blamed for the council and board of trustees not having been given a full explanation in their governance handbook. There is also the question of appointing any trustee with a special link to one of the countries who is likely to have the confidence of members there.*'

Tim Butler, the trust's solicitor, rejected my argument that the council could retain a fiduciary function in Ulster and went on to instigate legislation to give the trust's new trustees legitimacy across the water. It cost £150,000 to sort out Bernard Selwyn's point that the council had been left with a residual role in Northern Ireland.

At the trust's annual meeting, Sir William Proby implied the charity was prepared to buy land to thwart Government plans for three million homes in the countryside. I pointed out in *The Times* on 8 November 2007 ('National Trust chairman accused of hypocrisy for selling green-belt land') that the trust itself had disposed of 45 acres of land near Wimborne, bequeathed by landowner Ralph Bankes on his death in 1981. Though currently green belt its status was due for review in 2011. If planning permission is granted, the trust stands to make more than £20 million, under a covenant splitting the profit with the developer:

'*The chairman has made a speech about saving the green belt but it is a bit rich for him to be bleating now after they have been getting rid of acres of the land to speculative developers. It is blatant hypocrisy.*'

The odd thing about the council at this time was that it became increasingly determined to exercise powers which it had given away. It must have been frustrating for the new board to have so many of their decisions analysed and second-guessed by a somewhat stroppy council. In contrast I seemed both polite and supportive. The unnecessary duplication must have frustrated chairman Proby but he patiently sat out his final year. The standard of debate had deteriorated from Parliamentary committee quality in the 1990s to something on a par with what you expect to hear in Bournemouth Town Hall. The same applied to the addition of a morning session to meetings. We now covered less but in twice the time.

I prepared my exit strategy. At the 2008 annual general meeting I raised the problem of keeping faith with benefactors and donors. Details of those who had given land to the trust, or enabled it to be bought, used to be printed in the *Properties of the National Trust*. Known as the 'Green Book' this had not been revised since 1997. Nor was key information about those who provided public access being given on the ground. I quoted as an examples the information boards at Ebor Gorge in the Mendip Hills. These made no mention of the fact that 118 acres had been gifted by Mrs G. W. Hodgkinson, in 1967, in memory of Sir Winston Churchill. Such acknowledgements were a matter of courtesy and decency. They might also encourage future acts of altruism.

Sir William Proby stood down. Holding up a double-page spread from *The Times* of 22 November 2008, I welcomed Simon Jenkins to his first meeting as chairman of the National Trust:

> *'Hail to our new Caesar. As the survivor from the 1990 intake, who has served under five reigns, it is my pleasure to welcome Sir Simon Jenkins on your behalf. This Epiphany we have found a true leader, star and saviour, if this is any indication. "Trust me, we need more risk, less health and safety, says new chief." And so say most of us.'*

As an example of my practical backing for Simon's refreshing change of direction, I was quoted in the *Daily Telegraph*, having supported his proposal that we should accept the quirkily personalised No. 575 Wandsworth Road home of ex-Kenyan Treasury civil servant, poet and fretwork artist Khadambi Asalache. A rump of the council produced a report urging its rejection. Among other things, we were told, it was not representative of a British Empire connection. Something connected with the Indian sub-continent would be more appropriate. I countered with argument that not only was Kenya a typical British colony but the Victorians would have lapped up the image of the young Asalache, as a Masai herdsman, waving a spear as he read Shakespeare to his cattle:

> *'They would have seen him as the archetypal Noble Savage.'*

As for eccentricity, the trust already owned numerous white English follies, so a London house that had been turned into one by a black African would be in good company. Opposition melted when I raised the matter of 'unacceptable ethnic profiling' with the implication that I would invoke the 'r' word (for racism). Accepting the Asalache bequest did not preclude finding something Asian as well. The project went ahead but most council members seemed embarrassed rather than enthusiastic.

I had already decided how to mark my departure and issued a press release. In choosing the topical subject of risk aversion for my parting shot I was echoing what Simon Jenkins had been saying during his first year as chairman. Unknown to me at the time, this swan-song to the National Trust annual general meeting at Swindon, on 7 November 2009, had been given a whole page in that day's *Times* and was splashed across the top half of page three in the *Daily Telegraph*:

> *'With a landholding of 640,000 acres – which equals 1,000 square miles – we own the equivalent of one old-style English county. Therefore we must expect that one in 50 of national accidents, fatalities and headlines will happen on trust land. If we are lucky, that is.*
>
> *'The difference is that we advertise and encourage people to visit our land. Most counties contain their share of feudal estates that have spent the past 500 years keeping the public out. Much of this green and pleasant land is now*

being put behind new money fences, gates, walls and closed circuit television cameras that give the message "Keep Out" and "Go Away".'

I then made an allusion to the David Austin cartoon in the *Guardian* that had been inspired by my first such speech of 20 years earlier:

"NT" does not stand for "No Trespassing" [Applause].
'*We must continue to heighten our risk profile by inviting people to step on our land, fall into our lakes and rivers, and get clobbered by wind-borne debris from our 6 to 12 million killer trees. That's a conservative estimate. When Peter Nixon finishes counting them the total is likely to be more than 20 million of these accidents waiting to happen.*

'*Inside the great houses, American visitors get sniffy about mould, and think of terminal illness and calling their attorney if they find themselves entering a room that contains an antiquarian book. We should market aerosols with that distinctive National Trust smell. Or produce scratch-and-sniff perfume inserts for the wonderfully revamped and reborn* **National Trust Magazine.**

'*We own our liabilities "for everyone for ever". Hopefully there will always be people taking the risk of living by enjoying our properties. Because we are the National Trust it will always be a high-profile event when an accident inevitably happens. But things could be so much worse – Enterprise Neptune could have given us Beachy Head and we might also be caring for Brunel's Clifton Suspension Bridge* [Laughter].

'*Tell it as it is. Simon must be backed when he reminds Health and Safety bureaucrats and the media that if the nation wants the equivalent of an open house countryside then it will also have to accept the statistics that come with it. Otherwise they will restrict the landscape to visual access only.*

'*Risks also bring opportunities. As this government runs out of steam, there is one great conservation idea it failed to put into effect, during the 13 years when it had a chance. That is to experiment with re-wilding. Stop taking the moral high ground as every other nation on Earth gets rid of its iconic wildlife. We had eliminated most of ours, in the process of almost total deforestation, by 1000 AD.*

'*Bring back the beaver and lynx, and the European bison to Stourhead, plus the wolf in Scotland* [Applause]. *If there is no one else with the guts to propose it, let the National Trust do so, as nature's counterbalance to our own cuddly Pat Morris and his dormice and hedgehogs. Maybe the brown bear is a species too far but Paddington has great PR* [Laughter]. *It would certainly bring an element of excitement to visiting Trust countryside properties.*

'*Financially the 2009 implosion may also bring a unique opportunity. It offers the ultimate privatisation. Think boldly and put the National Trust investment portfolio into buying Whitehall for the nation. Then turn it into a nice little earner for as long as there's an England, by renting it back to the Government* [Applause].'

During my time with the National Trust I kept a watching brief for the interests of the Open Spaces Society. More sparingly, but often with impact, I took it upon myself to act as the conscience of the trust long before that was written into the governance script as one of the core purposes of the council. I could do it with special effect thanks to a direct link with the founders of the trust and the fact that as the Commons Preservation Society my predecessors were instrumental in giving more than 5,000 acres of common land and woods to the trust. Such interventions became unimpeachable when delivered with a suitable quote or paraphrasing of Octavia Hill, though avoiding co-founder Sir Robert Hunter as few had a clue as to his credentials.

As for the point and purpose of it all – now that council members are no longer trustees – we could no longer direct events or carry any responsibility beyond being a diffuse appointments body. We might now be seen as 'the conscience of the trust' but this turned into navel-gazing rather than discussing substantial management issues such as acquisitions policy or ethical (or unethical) investments. Like Britain in the post-war world, we had lost an empire without having found an alternative role.

Even the venues and hospitality went distinctly down-market. Best-ever accommodation was the Copthorne Hotel, Newcastle, to open the curtains to a premier footballer's view of the Tyne bridges. Equally good was the budget Holiday Express in Liverpool where over-sized Room 436 overlooks Albert Dock. Greatest disappointment was a seaside hotel in Brighton (not the Grand) with chronic over-heating. Retribution for that was to deposit a dead dogfish in the lift and listen for the scream. Then events were curtailed to a motel and a single day without dinner.

The fun days were over, as a National Trust insider confided, to Sherborne tree-surgeon Matthew Crabb:

'We used to have wine at our meetings but Rodney drank it all.'

-8-
Saving Open Spaces

Campaigning in Dorset ranged from highlighting the destruction of downland flora and ancient monuments by agricultural deep ploughing, and publicising cottage clearances on the Drax Estate at Morden, to taking on the Forestry Commission at Powerstock Common and British Gas and English China Clays in the Isle of Purbeck. I soon became the county spokesman for a catalogue of rural issues. The theme through the 1970s was saving the countryside, mainly waged through the press but briefly under the umbrella of the Council (re-branded Campaign) for the Preservation of (now 'to Protect') Rural England, until I resigned when its Dorset committee limply refused to endorse a nationally-promoted condemnation of stubble-burning on the grounds 'it might upset our farmers'.

I yearned for a national role which came when I found myself adopted as the protégé of veteran footpaths plaudit Mrs Ruth Colyer from Shillingstone who co-opted me as a committee member of the Open Spaces Society under chairman David Clark (now Lord Clark of Windermere), secretary Paul Clayden, and treasurer Sir Francis Boyd. It was fun to travel to London at a time when Britain's oldest national conservation organisation – founded as the Commons Preservation Society in 1865 – still had a rump of MPs and Lords who could book us rooms in Pugin's House of Commons or down in the mediaeval crypt beside Westminster Hall. By 1980 I was being groomed by Sir Francis as his successor. The means fell well short of the prestige as the society staggered into chronic deficit. My first task was to calculate whether we retained sufficient funds for paying redundancy moneys to the staff. Fortunately, old societies tend to have old members, and legacies kept us going for the rest of my stewardship.

Personnel changed fast. David Clark became Defence Secretary and Paul Clayden retired. Then, as treasurer, I doubled as acting chairman. In my annual report to the Open Spaces Society for 1988 I outlined the chaos out of which my chairmanship emerged. It was a year 'that started indifferently, and deteriorated' with Adrian Phillips of the Countryside Commission refusing us further funding for failing to fall in line with 'the grouse moor access issue' and the Society's energetic next secretary, Kate Ashbrook, was taken to task for 'high profile criticisms of key landowning organisations' that threatened 'the national consensus for legislation'. There had already been an unexpected walk-out from the annual general meeting by our chairman Guy Somerset from Exmoor, and the pro-tem appointment of Leeds solicitor Jerry Pearlman as his replacement, followed by the latter's sudden departure after the bust-up with the Countryside Commission. My summary of the year outlined how I came to be chairman and recalled the colourful meeting:

'If it is to be remembered at all in the annals of the society, 1988 will be the "year of the three Emperors". Where, perhaps, I disagree with the other two is that I do not regard the society's internal differences as having much significance. The theatricals of the 1988 annual general meeting were a poorly-scripted side-show.'

From being her henchman, I then had to contend with repeated requests from Mrs Colyer, including letters to the Charity Commission, claiming that the Open Spaces Society was in dereliction of its duty by not trying to upgrade public paths into byways open to all traffic. On 9 August 1990 I was able to write in *Blackmore Vale Magazine* that I had at last come across an adequate answer – that we were continuing to uphold our policy of 60 years ago, which was to keep motorised vehicles off green lanes. This editorial note appeared in the society's journal for October 1931:

'No one grudges motorists the use of public carriageways; but they in turn must realise . . . that walking and horse riding also are legitimate recreations which cannot be satisfactorily pursued on the same tracks as motoring.'

Unusually, in *Blackmore Vale Magazine* on 1 March 1991, I praised Dorset farmers Urban Stephenson and R. S. Doggrell (the latter wrongly, it turned out) for creating a network of two miles of new public paths across land at Stalbridge Weston:

'To say we are delighted is an understatement. I am amazed. Mr Stephenson has packed as many paths on his land as he can and he is an example to the nation – indeed he has done a better job of providing public access than you will find on the average National Trust land of similar size. If there were more farmers like Mr Stephenson and Mr Doggrell there would be no public access problem in this country. I just hope the walkers appreciate their kindness and that they don't have to pick up any litter or deal with other problems for their pains.'

The names had come from the minutes of the amenities committee of Dorset County Council but praising people can be a risky business. Mr Doggrell was not involved in Mr Stephenson's scheme and had not seen or signed any documents relating to it. More often my views discomfited fellow-travellers in the environment movement as with this letter in *The Times* on 10 December 1991:

'It is one of the travesties of environmental protection and values in the 20th

century that the Ministry of Defence has been the only agency to achieve the restoration of true natural wildernesses – vibrant with superlative ecology as well as shell-fire – across expansive scenery, such as on Salisbury Plain and the Lulworth tank gunnery ranges.

'Conservationists, however, have fought most of their rearguard actions to try to preserve uneconomic vestiges of decaying post-mediaeval agricultural landscapes. Many look very nice but are being sustained by human interference through costly management regimes.'

In Dorchester, a Dorset County Council spokesman was gracious enough to accept my protest on behalf of Open Spaces Society about 18 applications for rights-of-way which had been subject to 'chronic inaction' by its legal department for five years. One concerned a footpath from Wool to the River Frome which I claimed and won solely on documentary evidence. My wider concern was that the public was being prevented from using such routes. Because of the delay there would inevitably be fewer people who could come forward with evidence or memories at any inquiry. The spokesman's words were quoted by Chris Rundle in the *Western Daily Press* on 31 December 1991:

'What the society says is absolutely true. We have to put our hands up to it. It is just one of those jobs which tends to get put off and which no one got round to doing. We are in the course of publishing the first four routes and we hope to have the whole thing sorted out next year.'

The same day I had a letter in *The Times* pointing out that a report about threatened church and chapels was illustrated by a photograph of a rustic cob and thatch chapel at Cripplestyle, Dorset, which had since collapsed and was now a tiny garden:

'This is hardly the way we would wish to create an open space, but at least the spot has retained its quiet dignity and remains available as a place of pilgrimage, whereas several redundant Anglican parish churches in the same county were lost to the public on closure. They became "private chapels" for the owners of adjacent country houses.'

I then drew attention to England's biggest open spaces with an attack on the 'Moors Mafia' of grouse-shooting landowners who were pressuring the Government to abandon a Conservative commitment to provide access for air and exercise to registered commons. To register our 'grouse' we sent a brace of the birds to Mrs Thatcher in Downing Street. Tina Rowe quoted me in the *Bristol Evening Post:*

'I'm gunning for the powerful moorland mafia of earls, marquises and baronets who are trying to stop the commons being protected. There are not many of them but they have been running England for 1,000 years. The

Government had a manifesto pledge at the last election to give public access to all common land. There were plans to regulate commons with bye-laws which would have protected them.'

Giving a talk on 'campaigning for open spaces' to the annual general meeting of the Mendip Society at Blagdon on 16 March 1991, I rounded it off by criticising the Landmark Trust for being 'elitist' in preventing the *Balmoral* pleasure steamer from landing day-trippers on Lundy Island. The trust had a representative present to give a robust defence. Vic Dennison, in his report for the society's September newsletter, expressed surprise (if not admiration) for the efficiency of my publicity machine:

'What was intriguing about this controversy was that it was reported in the **Evening Post** *on the same day. Since the copy I purchased on my way home had been in the shop since 3 pm, well before the exchange had taken place ...'*

That used to be due to a close relationship with South West News. In more recent times it has continued through friendship with erudite Freemason and reporter Ed Baker and photographer side-kick Phil Yeomans at Bournemouth News and Picture Service. I've always had a reputation for producing good copy. Ed is strong on natural history and literary connections and Phil shares my enthusiasm for the Celts and antiquarian Dorset books.

Back in my own back yard, I castigated South Somerset District Council on the state of paths that had close encounters with the A303, as the *Western Gazette* reported on 25 June 1992:

'For six miles west of Wincanton not a single public right-of-way crosses the road properly. There's no way you can have a walk around these parts which involves crossing the road. While you are getting across the road you can't stop to work out where the path goes or you'll end up like a squashed hedgehog. These paths are so dangerous they're effectively never used by anyone.'

As a result the Leland Trail was diverted on to a bridge but otherwise the situation remains unchanged. Towards the Thames Valley, Greenham Common had the longest runway in Europe and was home for American cruise missiles, which were towed around the surrounding countryside until the collapse of Soviet Russia. Along with a hundred protesters, I then walked a token distance around the 9-mile steel and razor-wire perimeter (only a Mr Rendel completed the circuit), some time after the ladies of the Peace Camp had packed their bags. The Royal Air Force was handing the base to the Ministry of Defence land agent. There were fears that the Government would sell off all or part of the ground to developers when I addressed a 'Forbidden Britain' rally:

'Greenham Common has been stolen from the people. During the Second World War it was requisitioned for military use.'

Newbury Weekly News reported my speech, from beside the security fence at Crookham Common, on 1 October 1992:

'Two generations of Newbury people have been deprived of the right of taking exercise across more than a square mile of heathland. Greenham Common has already done its bit for Britain. This must now be our peace dividend.

'The land was bought by Newbury District Council for the people, for walking and recreation. It's their common land, and local people have registered their rights to graze animals and take sand and gravel from the common. The military has no excuse for keeping the land now. The Cold War has ended and the missiles have gone.'

I was there to support local Member of Parliament Mrs Judith Chaplin who had headed John Major's political office. Sadly, though only 53-years-old, she died on 19 February 1993. Our campaign was largely successful though there has been re-development around the edges.

Closer to home, in a feature on Wincanton for *The Visitor* magazine, I enraged brothers Ken and Roy Sansom of the Town Council by writing that mothers were up in arms about the local park after two youngsters cut their feet on broken glass. There were smashed bottles in the sandpit. I went on to describe it as 'an apology for a town park' with no shrubs, locked gates, no sign to tell the public who was responsible for it, and paths strewn with dog excrement. The brothers hit back with a petition from users praising the park, as Ken Sansom told the *Western Gazette* on 27 August 1992:

'All the playgroups have signed it to say how much they like taking the children there. It's very helpful to be slated because of all the people who have given up their spare time to work on it. We're not looking for bouquets but we want fair treatment.'

I managed to upset the rest of the town by asking for cobbles rather than car-parking in the Market Place and several tirades against the growing tide of litter from postmen's red rubber bands (which I pick-up and re-cycle) to the depressingly obsessive collection of a black plastic bag full of filth each week from a quarter-mile section of A303 verge. At the same time I pick, plant and spread wild flower seed and snip back competitive vegetation. An unintended consequence of having moaned about urban litter was that one of the responsible authorities (I'm now careful not to mention personalities) proceeded to cut down all roadside and car-park bushes and shrubs – whilst birds were nesting – on the rationale that rubbish is impossible to remove unless it can be picked-up from the ground.

Lord Kimball seemed to find my views dangerous when he quoted them in a House of Lords debate on 31 March 1991, as *Hansard* reported:

'I am certain that he is quite open when he sees the appointment of people from the Open Spaces Society as a way of achieving his avowed and published

Examining a tobacco plant,
photographed by Lynda White

Negotiating a stile,
photographed by Lynda White

Rodney Legg hacking his way across a
stile at Stinsford, drawn by Danny Byrne

Beside the lake at Holbrook House,
photographed by Joan Taylor

aim of curtailing agriculture in the national parks. He went on to say at the same time that in his opinion farming was no longer compatible with landscape conservation.'

From the macro to the micro, for the 130th birthday of the society in 1995, I re-found the remains of a stone seat to our founder, Lord Eversley, on the edge of land given to the National Trust in his memory, in 1928. When it was placed beside Hightown Common, in the New Forest, people walked there out of Ringwood along what is now the A31 dual carriageway. The trust had said the land itself was his memorial, but I found records of a seat having been carved in Purbeck stone and teak by Poole architect Miss Elisabeth Scott, who made her reputation by rebuilding the Shakespeare Memorial Theatre at Stratford-upon-Avon. The reason the trust's warden failed to find the seat was that it now lay on the wrong side of the fence beside a derelict bus-shelter in the roadside verge. It was agreed to have it moved to a nearby car-park and restored in time for a rededication ceremony.

When Radio-4's *Any Questions* came to Wincanton, mine was the quirky one at the end:

'I am allergic to white chocolate, Gardeners' Question Time, and subsidised farmers – who plough up rights of way and cost us more per head than the community charge! What does it take to make the panel sick?'

To my disappointment, Auberon Waugh failed to take the opportunity to choose something funny, and Emma Nicholson embarked upon a spirited defence of farmers. 'Bron' was much more fun when I saw him in a train to Taunton, and presented him with his full-page review in that night's *Evening Standard* – of which he was unaware – to be rewarded with gin and tonics in the bar. I told him that during the previous bit of bother down in the Persian Gulf, Plessey's marine division at Templecombe developed a mine-sensing device which they codenamed with the f-word and the name of the nation that the Americans love to hate. 'You can't call it that!' an executive barked; but they did, by spelling it backwards. The system was 'Narikcuf'.

One of my path claims in Dorset, for a short section of green lane on the side of Cobbetts Hill to create a link between Shipton Gorge and Innsacre, was won thanks to a German reconnaissance photograph from at Dornier Do.17P at 37,000 feet on 7 October 1940. It appeared across a page of the *Daily Mail* on 22 November 1996 ('How Adolf's pathfinder was the pacemaker'), having decided the balance of evidence lay in my favour, rather than with cattle farmer Peter Symes.

On 26 August 2002 I wrote a letter in *The Times* explaining the significance of an Act of Parliament a century earlier with the pioneering primary objective of safeguarding the view from Richmond Hill. On 4 June 2003 I followed it with one on the 'extra-City roles' of the Corporation of London including management of Hampstead Heath. Then, on 9 August, I defended the right of children to play out of doors after a 'No ball games' sign appeared in the public

Ball Court at Milborne Port, Somerset. It had been taken over by the Royal British Legion for a remembrance garden:

'It may have seemed appropriate at the time – utilising the last play-space of the teenagers who went to war – but, in putting it out of bounds, future generations of villagers were deprived of a purpose-built courtyard in which to play.'

On 19 June 2004 the *Western Daily Press* gave me a page ('Law takes a step in the right direction') in which to comment on a partial victory in which 54 acres of Cranborne Chase was ruled to qualify as access land. The article, which I dictated over the phone, involved a pair of A-list celebs:

'In some ways I can understand where Madonna and Guy Richie are coming from. Millionaires and celebrities have every right to be paranoid and feel the need to keep potential stalkers away from themselves and their families. Sadly there are a lot of fantasists out there and people like Madonna have every reason to want to keep themselves away from the public.
'But the land we are talking about is well away from Ashcombe House, Cecil Beaton's old place, which is screened by trees and impossible to get close to. The nearest a rambler could get to the house is at least a mile away. People walking across the land would be unable to sneak across its lawn and peek through windows of the house. The inquiry was never about people invading Guy Richie and Madonna's privacy, it was about opening up the British countryside to the public.'

From the depths of the countryside to the heart of the capital, my letter 'Naked streets' in *The Times* on 15 January 2005 made a point about a 'well-loved public open space' in Sloane Square being there for recreational use rather than as 'part of the highway'.

I presented a speech on green belts as the guest of the Campaign to Protect Rural England, when its Dorset branch met on the lawn beside Britain's oldest and biggest yew hedge, at Bingham's Melcombe House. I had a hand a little later in a story about that hedge (400 feet long, 30 feet tall and 30 feet wide, planted in 1550) which featured in *Daily Mirror* ('Yew missed a bit'), *Daily Mail* ('Yewmongous!') and the *Daily Express* ('It's about time yew had a haircut'). It actually comprises two parallel hedges:

'It is incredible – like a piece of architecture. There are openings in it so you can actually walk inside and see the ancient trunks and branches.'

Yew was planted by law in non-grazed churchyards and grounds to provide the shafts for longbows. They were cropped for Agincourt and Crecy. These days the trimmings from Bingham's Melcombe go a company in France that produces anti-cancer drugs:

'Yew is traditionally used for bow wood so it's ironic the clippings go to the French.'

Chunks from my talk beside the hedge appeared in the *Blackmore Vale Magazine* on 24 June 2005:

'Green belts have been a vital protective mechanism, but they do not reach out to the people. They should connect town and country, rather than divide them. Now green belts are becoming speculative land where the public is excluded. Our vision is for green belts where people are welcome, where they can wander freely and enjoy pleasant routes which link town and country.'

My utopian insight was for 'wildlife corridors' and 'riverside ribbons' to connect 'bungalow and bar in suburbia to hostelry and honeypot in the wider landscape'.

On 15 July 2005, Joanna Codd of the *Daily Echo* reported my views on countryside access for ethnic minorities, elderly people, city dwellers, young people and the disabled. 'White to roam?' was the punning headline. I told her that I had for years been criticising organisations like the National Trust and Open Spaces Society for being 'white, ageing and middle class'. On the ground I embarrassed councillors and wardens by targeting 'macho steps and stiles' which made access difficult for elderly and disabled people. Lady Kirk once told me that the problem with encouraging Asian people into the countryside was that to them it was perceived as a hostile place that was liable to be full of danger. Tigers must be rare in Yorkshire but I took her point:

'We have a cultural gulf that we've got to bridge before people from black and ethnic minorities feel at home in the countryside. To start with, we should turn back the nanny state and get school visits to the countryside reinstated. If we catch them young we can show them that the countryside is something to be enjoyed.'

Only one per cent of visitors to northern national parks are Asian or black. Even in the cosy south there is a powerful disincentive to exercising rights of access that embarrasses the native white middle classes as well as any potential ethnic users. Security paranoia is sweeping the land. Former rustic gems can be transformed in a month into miniature gated communities behind new-money grills, pillars and walls, with closed-circuit television cameras to monitor those who persevere along rights of way. The whole basis of public paths rests on a right to pass unchallenged along routes that cross what is otherwise entirely private land. That was always the case but it can now feel that you are both intruding and unwelcome.

My biggest single one-day splash across the national newspapers was on 20 June 2008 with before and after pictures of the iconic Cerne Giant which had become a 'green man' and merged invisibly into his mid-Dorset hillside. It soon shamed the National Trust into giving him a fresh coating of chalk. On 5 August 2008 I highlighted the 'yellow peril' of a flowering plant potentially lethal to horses, across a page of the *Western Morning News* ('Society issues warning about ragwort dangers'):

'In my 50 years of walking across Dorset I've never seen it so abundant. There are great swathes of it and it is very toxic and potentially very dangerous. It is catered for under the Weeds Act 1959 and landowners have to remove it if it becomes a problem. I always used to pull it up and take it away, but there is so much now it is not really worth it.'

That upset the entomological charity Buglife and the society's Kate Ashbrook, though she's been equally damning about bracken, which also has its ecological niche.

Publishing walks is even more fraught. The classic case for me came in 2002 when I was taken to task for photographing Fortnight Farm in the highly desirable and prosperous parish of Combe Hay in a deep-cut valley south of Bath. Why had I not asked permission to photograph their house, setting and dog Daisy on the lawn? How did I know the Labrador's name?

'The answer is firstly that I photograph buildings and their settings from the public highway, in this case a byway, and there is no copyright in either architecture or the layout of a garden. If, however, I wish to stray from the path or other public access land I would ask permission. On the course of a normal walk I use a couple of rolls of film so there would be considerable difficulties if I had to ask everyone for clearance. It is more than a matter of common courtesy. Secondly, having barked initially, Daisy joined me on the path and permitted me to take the liberty of reading her identification tag.

'As for the routes of the walk, we are criticised for compiling these from the map rather than seeking approval from farmers and other landowners. Here I react by saying that if I drive along the A30 or A303 I don't contact those living beside the road for permission to pass their properties.'

A category of countryside incomer that I am delighted to enrage is represented by those who erect new-money wrought-iron gates of the sort that pepper the prosperous hinterland of Manchester Airport. One particular set of four, with brick pillars, could be condemned with justifiable opprobrium as they were erected across a public path at South Petherton, near Ilminster. My comments appeared on half a page of the *Daily Mail* ('Ramblers' victory at the gates of wrath') and across six columns in the *Daily Telegraph* on 12 March 2009:

'They [the gates] *are totally out of place, ugly, incongruous, unwarranted, and completely excessive. It looks as if footballers' wives or lottery winners have just moved in.'*

The 'Agromenes' page in *Country Life* denounced my remarks as having 'the vulgarity of a Jonathan Ross interview'. The columnist hoped that Brian Herrick, the owner of the gates, would win his legal attempt to retain them 'simply on grounds of public rudeness and prejudice against private property'. The journal carried my reply on April Fools' Day in 2009:

'Agromenes is on great form spiking my credibility over utterances about the modern ornamental gates at Barcroft Hall. But whether they look monstrous or wondrous is not an issue. The dispute arose because they have been placed across a public highway rather than a private drive.'

My lasting achievement for public access was to successfully claim as 'open country' a total of 640 acres – a square mile of land – mainly in Dorset and Somerset. That was the net result as I had objected to far more having been left off the Countryside Agency's provisional maps. In fact I made more applications than the Ramblers' Association. Successes included Cadbury Castle and a scattering of slopes on the ridge of limestone downland southwards to Sherborne, plus Glastonbury Tor, the interior of Maiden Castle hill-fort, and a strip of heather on Brownsea Island.

I relished anything that justified the continued existence of the tiny Open Spaces Society in the shadow of the monolithic Ramblers' Association. Though accompanied in recent years by Tony Poyntz-Wright and now Di Hooley, with guest appearances from daughter Anna, I am by instinct a solitary walker who is repelled by the thought and sight of hiking groups. Cagoules and a choice of walking shoes (always the same old trainers for me) comes with an obsessive straight-ahead gait, oblivious to anything of interest on or beside the route. They cling to Baden-Powell's insistence on four miles per hour. I am pleased to average one mile per hour. Distractions and diversions include ancient monuments and other curiosities, flowers and wildlife, photo-opportunities that require a wait for clouds to pass, and obsessive clipping of overhanging vegetation.

'Ramblers celebrate victory', or such like, would be the heading, even when it was our success that was being acknowledged. They had monopolised the generic name in the media's mind. To others, however, collaboration was strength. There was silence when I pointed out that we were competing with the Ramblers' Association for donations, members, legacies and publicity.

Time for me had already been called by the Charities Act with its requirement that a management committee such as ours had to evolve into a board of trustees. Effectively, they would set the strategy, and put systems in place, but leave the staff to carry out the detail. Hands-off involvement did not appeal to this activist. Neither do modern ideas of governance encourage 20-year chairmanships. So I stood down on reaching that milestone in June 2009 and walked away from the Open Spaces Society.

–9–
Wheeler-dealer

As John Fowles was quick to realise, I am an instant intermediary in the supply of anything that happens to be in demand. That goes back to childhood, with seasonable fruit and vegetables being pulled round in the go-cart, and in different circumstances could so easily have been drugs or something equally illegal. In the event it evolved into antiquities and books. A natural magpie, I picked things up because I liked the look of them, and filled our Bournemouth homes at Easter Road and Headswell Avenue with stacks of books and boxes of fossils and Roman pottery. The first casualties were my toys. Victorian and Edwardian mothers were conditioned to give them away so that you could not revert to childhood.

More annoyingly was the disappearance of books that working class parents did not think were healthy for their children to read. The loss of Mau Mau 'Oath Ceremonies' is understandable. Other titles that vanished included libellous novels – rarities because most copies had been pulped – and a number of law books secreted among the juvenilia.

It now seems blindingly obvious but it took an age for me to accept that I could not keep everything. Reluctantly prioritising I reduced my personal collecting to three areas – Celtic stone heads, Dorsetiana and militaria. For a time I accumulated an alternative Dorset County Museum. In the 1970s the Second World War was considered too recent to qualify as history. Anything vaguely connected with either Thomas Hardy or T. E. Lawrence seemed destined to end up across the pond. Purist archaeologists here were uncomfortable with my Celtic tête-coupés and other discoveries, even though you cannot find stonework with a metal detector. The heads were featured in the *Sunday Telegraph* on 11 May 1997, though the dozen mentioned there have since bred profusely – to 189 at the last count   and are now even more of a presence:

'The fact they are so uncomfortably stiff, deformed and troubled because they are based on death heads is very discomfiting – but it adds to their power. The Celts collected the decapitated heads of their rivals as trophies, because they believed that every human attribute was contained within a person's skull and that by beheading an enemy they would inherit his powers. But real heads had a limited shelf life, which is why they began carving replicas in wood and stone. The wooden ones have rotted away, but the stone ones are very much in evidence throughout Europe.'

Roman carving of a
Sarmatian horseman,
in Purbeck marble,
from Bere Regis

Items passing through my hands have had a tendency to tell their own stories. One in particular sticks in mind. For a teenage project on the British Empire I borrowed an evocative old photograph from a boy at Winton Secondary School in 1963. It shows an expatriate in South America opening his post in the jungle, surrounded by copies of *The Sketch*, *To-day* and *Pears' Annual* for 1897. The boy's distant relation has a Colt revolver in his belt and machete at his side as he opens a letter. Unfortunately by the time I came across it again, I had long ago left school and forgotten who loaned it to me. So it was never returned.

Captioned 'A typical group 50 years ago', a studio photograph from Georgetown, British Guyana, was in an album I bought from Miss Beamish, an old lady in Parkstone. A colonial in the picture was identified as Jack Ismay, of the family from Iwerne Minster in Dorset, whose Joseph Bruce Ismay was chairman of the company that owned *Titanic*, and arguably responsible for the liner speeding into the iceberg. Coincidentally, there was another colonial, identical with the school friend's relation from the first picture.

There things stood until the advent of advanced digital scanners in 2003. Graham Hiscock at Camelot Photographic showed off his new kit by enlarging the letter in the ex-pat's hand, revealing not only a Victorian stamp but the full address, emerging from beneath a thumb:

'. . . *Haig Esq., 80 Hadfield Street, Georgetown, British Guyana, S. America.*'

The boy I knew with that name was John Haig (born 1949) who went on the school holiday to Devil's Bridge in mid-Wales. In those days he lived in the bungalow beside the River Stour at the end of Bridge Place, Northbourne.

The next coincidence came when I bought items of ephemera connected with Bohemiam artist Augustus John (1878-1961) who lived at Alderney Manor, Poole. Some had been in the possession of the ex-wife of Jack Ismay who may have been part of John's entourage. There were also three of Ismay's letters, beginning with one to 'My Darling Little Wife', dated 15 December 1911 and sent from the liner RMS *Empress of Britain*. He regretted not having thought 'to take the first photograph on my beautiful new camera of yourself and Peter'.

The next letter – to 'Dearest' – lamented their break-up on 'the most unhappy birthday that I have ever spent in my life', on 9 May 1912. Unhappiness had been triggered by Mrs Christiana Ismay's refusal to pose naked for a painting. 'Jock' Ismay was writing from Chalmers House, 43 Russell Street, London West Central.

His final letter – 'Dear Christiana' – was sent from The Holt, Canford Cliffs, Bournemouth West, on 10 March 1923. It confirms the arrangements for financing the schooling of their sons, Peter and John:

'It is not my intention to pay their travelling expenses to and from school, nor their clothing, as these are already provided by me in the allowance to you, and you are relieved of the expenses of their tuition.'

The book front could have its confessional moments. As I traded-up my personal copies of the county histories by John Hutchins and his later editors – a total of ten volumes – it was at the cost of conniving in butchering previous 'lesser' copies. These were knifed for their prints. Booksellers had become decorators – aided by colourists and framers – as they produced the fashionable wallpaper of the 1970s. Unethical but profitable.

My biggest profit, in percentage terms, was buying a first edition copy of John Locke's 1692 *Essay Concerning Human Understanding* from a local house-clearer who had just emptied a musty old cottage in Holwell. He asked £1. Christie's auctioned it for £3,000.

When, between 1980 and 1982, John Fowles did so much to inform and polish my transcriptions of John Aubrey's *Monumenta Britannica*, he refused any payment. So I bought an autograph letter at Sotheby's, signed by King Charles at Oxford on 11 February 1644, ordering Sir John Stawell at Taunton Castle to instigate the Civil War siege of Lyme Regis. This, as I mentioned earlier, I gave to the town's Philpot Museum of which Fowles was curator. Bartering art and antiques became something of a habit.

Pat Dunion recorded this 'We Hear' entry in *The Visitor* for February 1988:

'That the page rate for advertising in Mr Rodney Legg's next **Wincanton Directory** *is one 1832 spinning wheel.'*

1988 was the year of the Roman tombstones. Three are superlative. One came from Christie's Great Rooms but was too heavy to be taken upstairs, so it was displayed in the yard, where few potential bidders had noticed it. Marble, 70-cm high by 30-cm wide, it has a superb inscription:

D M [Dis Manibus] *THEOPAEDI FECIT EVPHENGES AVG LIB FRATRI BENE MERENTI* (*'To the spirits of the departed* [for] **this** [was] **made** [by] **Euphenges** [an] **Augusta freeman** [and] **most deserving of brothers'**).

That comes from the late first-century BC, probably from Turkey, but the other two are definitely Romano-British. In soft red sandstone, a stone from Deva (Chester) shows a man in short Roman dress holding a tankard, between pillars and an arch. His inscription, unfortunately, is almost worn away but he is almost identical to that for Acilius Avitus of the 20th Legion who came from Emerita Augusta (Merida) in Spain.

The third is definitely military. In Purbeck marble, found in a load of builder's hard-core at a development in Bere Regis, Dorset, it depicts a Sarmatian horseman with distinctive rounded hat. Again there is a similar stone in Chester Museum, as these auxiliaries were stationed in Lancashire in the 2nd century AD. In the case of my stone, it never travelled that far, having been broken in transit from the Purbeck quarries. It was then used as building stone. The horse and figure are virtually intact, however, as the *Western Gazette* reported on 6 January 1989:

'Mr Legg said he realised that the carving could not be mediaeval because of the horseman's rounded Celtic-style face and the absence of stirrups and other trappings from his mount apart from simple reins. He used hydrochloric acid to burn out the dirt [mainly **lime mortar**] *from the stone's background, but allowed the dirt to remain on the carving to make it stand out in relief.'*

For me the end of obsessive collecting was brought about by a combination of unwise sales, whilst I was mentally ill in the spring of 1993, and a burglary at my home which removed particular treasures. From that time the commitment was reduced to curating Celtic heads – soon to be the biggest single selection in captivity – in the hope that they will be accepted as a bequest to the British Museum; together with the Dorset material that has informed and inspired my researches. The result has been to inflict stacks of unsaleable books upon this little corner of the world. My favourite question is to be asked how many books I have written. 'Seven feet' is the answer – being the space they occupy on the office mantelpiece.

Not all was lost from the 1993 robbery. 'Stolen cranes restored – thanks to the BVM!' the *Blackmore Vale Magazine* reported on 13 August 1993. They happened to be dead-ringers for a pair in the Larmer Tree grounds at Tollard Royal (not that landowner Michael Pitt-Rivers had nicked my pair). The magazine told the story and photographed me with the cranes and WPC Wendy Whitfield who re-united us in Wincanton:

Vickers-Maxim machine gun last used by Nationalist Chinese, photographed by Roland Gant

Rodney Legg surrounded by Celtic heads, photographed by John Baxter

'Sharp-eyed readers may think they have seen these cranes before. So did writer and publisher Rodney Legg when he saw the striking picture by Dave Penman on our front page a couple of weeks ago. And so did someone at Yeovil police station who thought they were identical to a pair they had in their recovered property section, which had been found in an estate car in St Michael's Road, Yeovil.

'The police contacted us – and so did Rodney, who had an identical pair stolen from his home near Wincanton in April, while he was in hospital. We were able to put Rodney and the police in contact and he was reunited with his beautiful sculptures.'

Coincidentally, I was also robbed from my rooms on Steep Holm island, but those buccaneers only relieved me of a defective radio and a few rusty tools. Of more consequence was £100 damage to a door and its frame. I commented on the theft in the *Western Daily Press* on 11 October 1992:

'I don't know what they were expecting to find but they must have been pretty disappointed to go to all the effort of breaking in and just get what they did. We really are a shoestring operation and none of the stuff on the island is worth the effort of being lugged down the cliff.'

In recent years I only bought and sold on a small scale but several of my finds have received national attention. One, given by favourite aunt Effie Watts – who had it from cousin George Hardy in Wareham – had a page in the *Daily Express* and its picture across five columns of *The Times* on 3 August 2005. It was a gold and sapphire-mounted plait from Lord Nelson's queue, taken by flag-captain Thomas Masterman Hardy after the hero's death on winning the Battle of Trafalgar, presented to one of his servants. It later came back into the possession of the Hardy family, together with a copy of *The Times* from 10 January 1806, recording Nelson's funeral, and a splinter of oak from HMS *Victory*. A note accompanied the memento:

'A lockett of the hare of Lord Nelson gived to my husband by Admirel Hardy for his loyal servis. Jane Long, West Millton.'

My ancestor James Legg (1798-1860), born in Powerstock, was a thatcher at West Milton. George Hardy, from whom I've also inherited collections of clay-pipe bowls and Dorset fossils, was a reclusive magpie.

His example encouraged me to accumulate the best collection of museum-quality Romano-British Hamstone carvings in captivity. Forgetting eight Celtic heads – because they belong with my collection of heads that is destined for the British Museum – there are a couple of altars, with one inscribed to the tree-god Silvanus ('DEO SILVANO TA'), four stones with figures, and a stone draughts' board (with three white and seven black pottery disc) 'Given by Lord Ilchester, 7 March 1938'. Hamstone came and comes from Ham Hill, above Stoke sub Hamdon and Montacute and was far from river and sea communications, so it has limited distribution across south Somerset and north Dorset.

Three of the four stones with figures represent the 'Genni cucullati', who were a brotherhood of wise men in cloaks and cowls, the hood being known as the 'cucullus'. They may also be the originals for the magi of the Christmas story in the Bible. One of my mysterious characters is holding an object that might represent a severed head. I have a fourth carving holding a staff, bought in Carlisle, in buff sandstone from beside Hadrian's Wall. The largest of my pieces features a frieze of three such figures, though one has been largely washed away, which was rescued from the River Yeo, near Bradford Abbas. A Roman marching camp was discovered on the nearby hill in the drought of 2010.

Similar carvings have been found near Roman military sites in Gloucestershire and Northumberland. Winter has also been represented as a hooded man. Rather surprisingly, one of my carvings was photograph in the *Sun* ('Hoodies roamed our past') on 14 November 2008 with my comment:

'They are mysterious, sinister and masculine.'

At a car-boot sale at Shepton Mallet in 2009 I came across an example of anthropodermic biblioplegy which is the use of human skin for binding books. The tattooed remains of a Victorian pocket book, preserved in oil in a medicine bottle, came with a box of military books and was accompanied by a letter from a member of the Egerton family, written at Stafford Rectory, Dorset, in 1896. West Stafford is just one parish away from Stinsford and Dorchester where novelist Thomas Hardy was turning such macabre tales into his Wessex novels.

Six square inches of skin with the faint trace of an anchor – indicating a sailor – features a wedding tattoo. It shows female (left) and male figures facing and greeting each other, and initials below for 'MS' and 'ED'. He smokes a long-stemmed churchwarden pipe. The scene is probably British and certainly European. An explanatory letter, on black-edged mourning stationery, sent from Stafford Rectory on 24 March 1896 is addressed to 'My dearest Frankie':

'I know how pleased you will be to learn that I have only this morning discovered the long lost pocket book made out of the skin of the man who shot your father! I had in vain looked for it before.'

Signed Blanche, the letter was from Mrs Caroline Egerton. She came across the pocket book whilst clearing the rectory following the death of her father, Canon Reginald Southwell Smith, in December 1895. He had been rector of West Stafford for almost the entire Victorian period, from 1836 till his death. Howard Pell has researched the Egerton family for me. Egertons, and their Grey-Egerton line in particular, have long associations with both Dorset and the military. Distinguished members include several Major-Generals, a Vice-Admiral and a Field-Marshal, plus Ambassadors and a colonial Governor.

Blanche Egerton (born Caroline Blanche Southwell Smith) recorded the incident in which the skin-man was killed and flayed in an example of summary justice. The wife of Colonel Caledon Philip Egerton, she penned her 'Recollections' in an unpublished manuscript now preserved in Dorset Archives at Dorchester:

'Behind the green and beige doors of the bookcase of my mother's bedroom was one of the most gruesome of all her possessions. It was a pocket book made out of the skin of man who had attempted the murder of my uncle Major Simpson in the Chinese War.'

This was the first Opium War of 1839. It is recorded in *The London Gazette* that William Henry Simpson, born in Hampshire in 1806 and serving with the Madras Rifles, was 'severely wounded' during the capture of Chin-Keang-Foo on 21 July 1842. He returned to Calcutta on the *Tennaserim* from Nanking after the signing of the treaty in August 1842. By 1851 he was aide de camp to Major-General Sir Hugh Gough who had led the British campaign in China.

'Dearest Frankie' of the letter was third son, Francis Blake Simpson, who was born in 1859 and went to Harrow School where he was tutored by Blanche's elder brother, Boswell, and followed his father into the Army. The current head of the family, 95-year-old Major-General Sir David Boswell Egerton – 16th baronet in a line created in 1617 – told me in December 2009 that he had no knowledge of the skin and had never heard of Major Simpson:

'I can't think why anyone should want such a relic.'

Of all the Battle of Britain memorabilia that I have bought and sold there is one item I always retained and shall bequeath to Dorset County Museum. Some of the items were acquired at a time when the Second World War was regarded as 'too recent to be history' but now bits of old clothing and crumpled engines have started to appear in collections. My special find, however, is much more evocative.

That relic is the windscreen of Spitfire N3173 of 152 Squadron, from RAF Warmwell, near Dorchester. It comprises a 25-mm thick sandwich of two sheets of reinforced glass with a membrane of plastics between them. The top has the semi-circular exit hole of a cannon shell that passed through the seal between the windscreen and the cockpit. The shot was fired from a Heinkel bomber at noon on 25 September 1940 as the crippled aircraft ploughed into the ground at Church Farm, Woolverton, near Frome. Bomber and the fighter crashed at the same moment.

Heinkels had devastated the Bristol Aeroplane Company's works at Filton and were heading back to their base in France. Flying the Spitfire was 20-year-old Kenneth Christopher 'Casie' Holland. I researched the story for Diarmuid MacDonagh and the *Dorset Echo* of 5 October 2010:

'This must have been a unique case because the planes shot each other down and crashed into the same farm just 500 yards apart. The Spitfire shot the bomber then went after it to check it was finished, but incredibly the rear gunner got a shot off. By a sheer fluke it penetrated the seal between the toughened-glass windscreen and the air-frame, glancing across the scalp of the pilot.

'Both planes came down in Church Farm and all were killed apart from the bomber pilot. The Spitfire pilot died before he could get to hospital. A plaque was erected on the farm and gave the Spitfire pilot's name as Ripley, which was confusing because his name was Holland. It turned out that he was an Australian orphan from Manley in Sydney. The name Ripley was that of his guardian in Camelford, Cornwall.

'He was having a busy September, having been credited with half a Junkers Ju.88 bomber shot down on the 17th, and full credit for the kill of another Ju.88 on the 19th. On the 25th his mistake was to go down for a closer look after the pilot parachuted out. His loss brought the squadron's death-toll to seven and that for the station at Warmwell to 15. Twice that number were killed before the Battle of Britain was over.'

Other artefacts from the crash-site were auctioned locally and I have acquired Casie's goggles and the mouth-piece of his wireless transmitter. His squadron shared Warmwell – the only Battle of Britain airfield between Eastleigh and Exeter – with 609 Squadron and I have their shove-ha'penny board along with other contemporary souvenirs of our 'finest hour'. Poignantly, the Dorset site representing the greatest action that saved this nation is now gravel pits, caravans and suburbia, but there is still a row of dispersal bays set in the edge of Knighton Heath Wood beside beech trunks that still carry graffiti for 152 and 609 Squadrons.

After finding miscellaneous machine-guns I acquired a wartime 40-mm Bofors anti-aircraft gun from Port Talbot. That's a truck-sized bit of kit with a 12-feet barrel. I challenged Roger Cuss, running a car recovery service from Wincanton, to deliver it to RNAS Yeovilton. From there it was air-lifted by Sea King helicopter to Split Rock Battery on Steep Holm which still possessed a circle of bolts on which one of these guns was emplaced in 1941. That was my largest item of bric-a-brac.

On the other end of the scale, still living with me, sits an incredibly life-like marble head of Emperor Galba who ran Rome for a brief summer in AD 69. He was a Christmas present from myself in 1982. Servius Sulpicius Galba, with same strong profile as his coins, cost a couple of grand and came as the reward for writing *Romans in Britain* which I treated as an adventure story. He still brings me pleasure, as do contemporary antiquities from Dorchester, which have accumulated as a virtual alternative Dorset County Museum.

In a Sea Fury at RNAS Yeovilton, photographed by Tony Goddard

–10–
Personally Speaking

Having moved to Milborne Port, near Sherborne, I set about upsetting the villagers with banner headlines. Ian Hunter reported in the *Western Daily Press* on 26 August 1971:

> *'A parish council meeting in Milborne Port collapsed in uproar last night when members were told they were meeting illegally. It happened after they were accused of trying to conceal plans for new homes. The meeting had been called to discuss detailed confidential development plans loaned to the parish council by Wincanton rural council. They were for 57 private homes in South View, Milborne Port.*
>
> *'No public notice was given of the meeting. Postcards were distributed by hand notifying councillors only. Under the Admission to Meetings Act, notice must be given of time and place of a meeting at least three days before. And by law all parish council meetings must be open to press and public.*
>
> *'The uproar broke out after Rodney Legg, aged 24, editor of the* **Dorset County Magazine**, *stood up and told the council:* "You cannot make any decisions or act on any decisions you make tonight."
>
> *'The chairman, Mrs Anne Wilkins, said:* "I'm completely flummoxed. There was no intention to exclude members of the public. There have been some objections to the extent of new developments in the village." *But councillor Edward Cookson, a parish councillor and member of Wincanton rural council admitted that with members of the public present at the meeting, the plans could not have been discussed properly and would not have been available for inspection.'*

The story resumed in the following day's paper with Mr Cookson leading the rebuttal:

> *'There were no secret meetings at all. If Mr Legg is talking about brushing things under the carpet, there is no carpet in the council chamber. He is a trouble maker. We have discussed some things in private, but we are entitled to do so.'*

The media, however, likes mavericks who stand up for the right to report. The leader column in the *Western Daily Press* took up this 'Lesson in law':

'Naturally, the parish councillors were displeased with the intervention. It would have been impossible for them to have discussed the confidential documents, they said, with members of the public present. But that is no excuse. It is bad enough that we should have to tolerate exclusion from councils which have the right to do so, without having to accept the same treatment from councils which have not.'

Heavy snow and strong winds on Saturday 18 February 1978 resulted in most roads in Dorset and south Somerset becoming impassable by late evening. The great myth that emerged from melting drifts in the middle of the following week was that of 'the body in the snow'. It was a story that erupted spontaneously in bars and shop queues. The gist was always the same, but the location floated across the hills, being two villages removed from the place in which it was being told. Young printer Stephen Taylor reported from Milborne Port:

'The father of a chap a friend of mine knows at Stalbridge, dug a body out of the snow. The arms were poking up through the drift.'

My neighbour Julie Paniccia heard the same story, though the place had drifted, when she made it through the melt-waters to the village stores in Charlton Horethorne:

'We heard about the body that was pulled out of the snow by the boys who live next to you.'

That was the *Dorset* magazine team of Colin Graham, Malcolm Noyes and myself. The story contained a grain of truth. On the Sunday morning we trudged for half a mile along the paralysed A303 dual carriageway to a cluster of vehicles on the top of the hill above Sparkford. I thought I had found a body. Slipping and sinking into mammoth 15-feet drifts, and finally learning to crawl across the soft top of the snow with my spade horizontal – to displace body weight – I reached a stranded Spillers-French delivery van engulfed in fresh snow. There was a heap of the stuff ominously across the driver's seat and in a mound over the floor.

I put my spade through the side window of the van and prodded the shape. It contained the driver's coat, glasses and shoes. The fine, dusty white-stuff that curved across John Miller's cab in body-pose had come from every crack in the side of the van that the Arctic wind had found. Finally, I used the spade to smash the rear lock, to make sure its driver was not collapsed in the back. The man himself, luckily, had made it out of the snow and back home across the fields to North Cadbury.

Meanwhile, across the road, Ernest Paniccia and Colin Graham were at another truck. Peter Williams of Willesden (travelling under his trade-name, Peter Prince) had a van filled with mobile disco equipment and had been fleeing

Above: *Last family outing of Ted, Barrie and Gladys Legg, to Woolbridge Manor in the mid-1960s, photographed by Rodney Legg*

Above right: *Rodney Legg on the county line, at Woodyates, photographed by John Pitfield in 1982*

Right: *Stand-in barman, at Holbrook House Hotel, photographed by Joan Taylor*

Below left: *At the Roman Town House in Colliton Park, Dorchester, photographed by John Pitfield*

Below right: *Rodney and Salman Legg, en route to Steep Holm, photographed by John Pitfield*

a show for 600, cancelled at the Johnson Hall in Yeovil, when he slid to a halt against a wall of snow. Peter and his electronics man, Christopher, were used to sleeping rough in the van (quite comfortably, as it was packed with blankets and sleeping bags) but that morning they were intensely cold.

Snow had welled up through the engine and into the cab. Peter and Christopher had to be cajoled to gather themselves in protracted slow motion for the walk to safety. Neither were their rescuers in much better shape. I had to drag myself to the leeward side of the van to plead for a blanket. Reaching the first van had filled my boots with snow and my feet were now immobile. The staggering home was to be in the face of an easterly Force Ten gale that was lifting the finely powdered snow off the fields and hurling it across the empty white wasteland that should have been the dual carriageway.

Braver souls stayed on. Robert Spiller, a stubby Royal Marine bandsman from the Royal Yacht *Britannia*, coaxed a bearded man from a purple Marina. He then beckoned down a passing Yeovilton helicopter to check for life in two other smothered cars. An officer was winched down, waved a negative, and left sticks poking out of the snow to show the sites of the cars. Robert neglected to salute.

One of the cars belonged to the Royal Naval Air Station. The dark green BMC 1800 had been abandoned in the middle of the night and its driver hitched a lift with Military Police – operating two Land Rovers – which were the last traffic along the A303 until snowploughs broke through on the Tuesday. When he arrived at Yeovilton he was asked where he had left the car, and found it impossible to give an answer, as by that time everywhere looked the same. His interrogator was unforgiving:

'Christ, you can't just leave a Ministry of Defence car, under any circumstances. And you haven't just left it somewhere, you haven't a clue where you put it.'

When they got that one back it had a line of dents battered along the roof. Sightseers from Blackford village had arrived on the hilltop and walked their dogs across the frozen drifts. An oasis of green rooftop was one of the precious few signs that survived of life as we knew it. Not that we were in any way exceptional. In fact, unlike many, we retained throughout the three basics of civilised living (electricity, telephone and water) and could listen to a constant stream of 'What's Off' on Radio Solent in case we had any expectations of attending evening classes in Bournemouth or the Monday cattle market at Sturminster Newton.

Our second bout of body searching came three days after the blizzard when with traffic warden Bill Cox from Wincanton, we poked bamboo canes into an endless drift, searching for a missing Mini. It was only after Bill said the man had left his car 'on the road from Castle Cary to Holton' (which was a mile away) that the exercise was terminated. Back at the house, mildly disappointed with the anti-climax, it was Peter Prince who unwittingly germinated the great myth of the blizzard in the West:

'Go out and find me a body sticking out of the snow, so that we can at least go back to London and have something to show for our week.'

During a few years in Milborne Port, Colin Graham and I turned the delicensed Railway Inn (which has now reverted to its earlier name of Angel Inn) into the village youth club. One of the young lads from around the corner, Stephen Taylor, not only learnt to drive with us – before he could apply for his licence – but soon started printing my books and magazines. He now trades as Wincanton Print Company and has global customers, and I defended his initiative in the *Visitor* magazine for January 1989:

'Whilst I can think of no Wincanton building of recent times that is likely to win the Prince of Wales Award for Architecture I think it a bit harsh that you single out that of Wincanton Litho for special condemnation. Its brick-clad sides are a quantum leap from the tin-can degradation of Bennetts Field.

'Standing as it does in splendid isolation the new printing works attracts undue attention. Soon, sadly, it will be surrounded by other structures that are less imposing. Wincanton Business Park sounds fine but it is going to need more than a prestigious name to prevent the onset of tackiness.'

Litho, incidentally, is the Greek word for stone. That used to form the bed for letterpress printing but it tends to be a little obscure for the Somerset mind. When I stood in to answer the telephone the most enigmatic variation for a business name 50 miles inland was 'Wincanton Lifeboat'. I was asked to order some 'Vellum' (paper) and provided the phone number for an abattoir (vellum is goat skin). Stephen Taylor did at least laugh but partner Andrew Johnstone was not amused. I once took Stephen and a couple of spades to Land's End in a blizzard to dig around the Blind Fiddler standing stone after wrongly interpreting clues to the spot where Kit Williams buried a golden hare for his *Masquerade* puzzle-book.

Some of the exploits were shared with Kenneth Allsop's daughter, Mandy, to whom I was briefly engaged in 1974 but to my ageing mother's disappointment the concept of marriage became anathema. I always was the source of my own problems. My rather belated discovery of sexuality – benefiting from legalisation during my lifetime – grew in complexity. It has been expressed and shared through long-term friendships rather than close-proximity living. There is more pleasure in being a visitor to other people's lives than comes from indulging my own. Relationships with cats are about all I can offer at home. Once I escape through the door, however, my inherent impatience soon delivers distractions.

In Wincanton town I rashly supported the enhancement scheme for the Market Place and objected to 'laissez-faire parking on the Alan Mann memorial cobbles'. Mayor Mann had undertaken a £23,500 heritage enhancement scheme. Actually they were not 'cobbles' but recycled York stone sets. It was a crater-like landscape across which disadvantaged persons stumbled in order to form an orderly queue as Malcolm and Nigel McCormack provided 'free money' in the Post Office. There were falls and damaged limbs. I further muddied the debate by finding a royal charter from the time of Mary Tudor and then mixed her up with Mary, Queen of Scots. The former lost Calais and made the Channel Tunnel inevitable; the latter merely lost her head. 'People cannot help their ignorance', someone helpfully pointed out. It's surprising how many people care about a couple of old queens.

I had New Year blues in issue No. 86 of *The Visitor*, five years after Michael Heseltine stormed out of the Cabinet over the issue of who should own the biggest factory in Yeovil (which dates it to 1990):

'Despite a little local difficulty down at the petrol pumps, the world continues to drift toward peace, jeopardising helicopter production in Yeovil (unless of course we go and lose the lot taking out the Garden of Eden up the Euphrates). One wonders if any of this could have happened if Leonid Brezhnev had been kept on the drip for a couple of decades.'

That winter I had an out-of-body experience. It was about 02.00 hours and I was in bed with pneumonia. I felt intensely cold and lost all power to move. My teeth chattered out of control with the jaws hammering together. Then I was looking down at myself, lying naked on the bed with the cat curled up at the bottom, with everything in the room in perfect perspective for a view from the ceiling including dust and papers on top of the wardrobe. Then the fever stopped. What followed it was the most gorgeous warmth I've ever experienced. I sank into a deep sleep from which it was with some surprise and disbelief that I awoke to find that I was alive and it was time to let the cat out in the morning.

Having been forced northwards by increasing property prices, from Shillingstone to two Milborne Port addresses, and then into that hilltop cottage beside the A303 at Maperton, I again took on the local community. It is a parish of two halves, with the main road being the dividing line, and I found myself at the sharp-end through the decade before the advent of mobile phones. Broken-down motorists and accident victims (some covered in blood) were a monthly occurrence, at all times of day and night, to use my land-line to contact the emergency services.

The principal cause was an intersection on the brow of the hill, above Blackford Hollow, with minimal visibility. Of the crashes within sight of my house, two remain in mind. In one a drunken company director turned into the wrong lane on the dual carriageway and wiped out himself and a Gillingham schoolteacher. In another a young driver with worn tyres – 'safer on a dry road than those with a tread', I was told by the police – rammed into the back of a mother driving her young son westwards into a blinding sunset. They died and the boy's toys were strewn along the verge when I took an insurance assessor to the site.

So I am relieved to say that I played a role in having the intersection closed. Resistance was represented by our *Excalibur* parish magazine which gave the official address where residents could write with details of inconvenience experienced since the cross-roads was sealed. My backlash was published in the *Blackmore Vale Magazine* on 14 August 1992:

'Instead of putting a price on those little detours it has caused us, it would be more in keeping with practical Christianity to reflect on how much grief is being saved by this belated contribution to road safety. That's the obvious topic for a sermon. No one who used it other than at well selected rare moments of under-use can have failed to realise that it was lethal.

'Such intersections, particularly on a hilltop, were outmoded by the time this one was built, and the fault lies partially with the local councils at the time for clamouring for what amount to lavish farm subways rather than urging properly located underpasses that would be usable by general traffic. Environmental road assessments and the models of traffic flow are proving to have been grossly inadequate. Improving roads such as the A303 brings all kinds of unexpected effects to the surrounding countryside. Lucky Blackford has become a backwater, but many more former quiet places near the A303 now take much of the traffic for which the main road was originally designed.'

I was also taking Fisons to task for peat-digging on the Somerset Levels and describing Wincanton as 'a riot-torn town' after having my front doors kicked in by binge-drinkers returning home in the early hours after enjoying recently-extended licensing hours. Thank you, Mrs Thatcher.

My lasting contribution to Wincanton pub culture has been the sign of Uncle Tom's Cabin in the High Street. Red-nosed cider drinking locals claimed it for one of their own (with a yokel being depicted on the sign) rather than a black Southerner with a young white girl on his knees. Publican Thomas Green named the thatched hostelry for Harriet Beecher Stowe's famous novel when news reached England of the firing of the first shots in the American Civil War in 1860. The conflict was said to have been triggered by the famous anti-slavery novel. Genuine iconography was restored in time for the election of the first Afro-American president.

In an on-going study of the enigmatic life of Colonel T. E. Lawrence, the latest and fullest version being *Lawrence of Dorset,* I published in full the coroner's notes of his inquest in 1935, together with quotes from intelligence officer Colonel Richard Meinertzhagen's diary which had remained secret in Rhodes House Library in Oxford. The former contains Corporal Ernest Catchpole's evidence of seeing a black car passing Lawrence immediately before he fell to his death from his motor-cycle. The latter confirms that Lawrence was 'Director-Designate' at the time of a proposed amalgamation of the British security services.

Then came personal information that motor-cycle manufacturer George Brough had found traces of black paint on Lawrence's machine. To add to the mystery, Lawrence was being groomed to meet Hitler on behalf of fascist intellectual Henry Williamson, and there were the first stirrings of Jewish Irgun terrorism. The speculation was splashed by Alun Rees across a page of the *Daily Express* ('Did MI5 assassinate Lawrence of Arabia?') on 3 July 1995. My conclusion certainly stretched the probabilities:

'My opinion is that there is now an overwhelming weight of evidence pointing to the fact that he was assassinated.'

I went through a final fling of twentieth-century correspondence and haven't written a personal letter since. Incoming letters were from Gerald Pitman in Sherborne and Merle Chacksfield in Swanage. My outgoing therapeutic series went to Sam Rock, when she was a student in Birmingham, and Debbi Callaghan (nee Lachter), teaching geography in Reading. Weekly visits were made to my adopted family in Sherborne, namely the tribe gathered by Matthew Crabb and Julia Thornicroft-Taylor. Julia reproved me when I climbed a traffic regulation pole to show Ben and Ollie how to do it:

'You are 45-years-old but you act like a hyperactive child!'

Julia and Matthew mastered the intricacies of providing Christmas dinner. I reciprocated by picking unwanted sprouts – the best bit of meal – from Ben's plate. By inclination I'm veggie but I fudge this by liking game and shell-fish. The ethical justification is to avoid anything from an abattoir 'because I don't eat pets'. That 'short, free life' argument fails to impress fundamental vegans, such as Martin Bull of the National Trust, even though I was the 'me too' loud-mouth who ensured he received special needs. I would slap others across the wrist as they reached for our gourmet plate:

'Hands off – this is ours! All that stuff over there is for you carnivores.'

Two other collections of friends surrounded Karen Eden in Wincanton (who moved to Bristol to become Mrs Richard Wike) and Bill Hoade plus Pip Oakes-Ash and family in Wimborne. My other outing has been to see John Pitfield once a week. The lasting memory of Karen in Wincanton is that she arranged for red-haired Mr Simon's unisex hair salon to turn my hair blue in November 1987. To Mrs Joan Taylor at Holbrook House Hotel, my evening watering hole for two decades, it looked like 'a badly adjusted television set'. People asked about it – 'so we won't make the mistake of going there' – to the extent that Simon Richfield made it clear that he was not 'that sort of hairdresser'. Before and after it has been clearly evident that I generally cut my own hair though Di Hooley now tries to make me presentable (an impossibility). I miss Mum most for the absence of her customary greeting as she advanced with the implement in question:

'Comb your hair, Rodney.'

The working day is split between long bouts on the screen (dull days) or perpetual motion across the county (sunny days). My eyesight held up, without glasses, for long distance spotting of boats and deer. Those brown eyes, inherited from my mother, once zoomed in on a document in the hands of an Army officer at the other end of a long table at Lulworth Camp. He realised I was studying it:

'You can't read that from here?'

So I did – every word, figure and punctuation. He was impressed.

'That's classified!'

Part-time lecturing on interviewing techniques, at Weymouth College in the 1980s, led to lectures on editing and publishing in media studies classes at Bournemouth University three decades later. As a distraction from writing books I have sent letters to the national press, usually *The Times*, where my first eleven appeared intermittently between 1973 and 1990. They show an inherent eclecticism that I strive to maintain – Army ranges at Lulworth; Art as an investment; Island reserves; Avoiding a toss-up; Maze hunger strikers; Ploughing Dorset's archaeology; Saving Malta's heritage; Blocking of footpaths; Legal view of highways and byways; Birds and glass; Restrictions on right to roam. Ten were self explanatory. 'Avoiding a toss-up' was about distinguishing 'legal' and 'illegal' bulls in fields crossed by public paths.

The next six were on the heritage theme – Farmers and landscape; Cripplestyle Chapel; Fate of Max Gate; Saving pillboxes; Mapping paths; Preserving trees. Then came three in which I took a special pride, particularly for my 'World of their own' which took the humorous bottom right-hand corner of *The Times* letter-page on 22 December 1995:

'It comes as no surprise that Mr Sallit has located another planet (report, December 11). I know a number of the people who live there.'

With a missive on 'Floral tributes' I came to terms with the loss my mother, Gladys Norah Legg, to bowel cancer at the age of 91. There had been correspondence about funeral flowers:

'Non-floral death tributes, in the form of charity cheques, can also come with pretty cards and kind words. The bonus, as I have found after my mother's recent funeral, is that her favourite animal rescue centre has benefited by £310. In the last week I have been able to drive past Ray Joliffe's field of donkeys at Poole with pleasure of knowing that my mother has been feeding them through the recent snow. She would have liked that.'

Another subject close to my heart – 'Pub names' – appeared on 22 July 1996:

'Loss of historic inn names is nothing new. Milborne Port, in south Somerset, currently offers the choice between the Queen's Head on one corner and the King's Head on another; but until 1817 or thereabouts the latter was known as 'The Tippling Philosopher' – surely the best pub name in the land?'

Others must have thought so, as it has been reinstated. Later in the year I was explaining 'Jude's obscure origins' (in Berkshire rather than Dorset) and writing on the 'South Downs at risk'. In a 'Rock too far' on 20 June 1997 I protested against the violation of remote Rockall by a plastic capsule in a Greenpeace stunt. 'Drink and health', on 25 September, was a tribute to the newspaper's veteran doctor:

'Many of us are increasingly indebted to daily doses of Dr Tom Stuttaford. Seeing his name each morning reminds me to take a "blood-thinning" aspirin tablet. His articles, including extracts from his book on alcohol, provide a welcome antidote to half a century of censure against life's little enjoyments. At last there is reassurance that moderate indulgences are not only good for us (physiologically as well as psychologically) but promise to be lifesaving.

'As for the measure, it is hardly to be regretted that two to four glasses of claret a day, with food, may well prove to be more effective than drinking just one. Cheers to our greatest guru.'

Salman, for a cat, is not a neutral name. I was unaware, however, that it is a desert town in Iraq, until Pentagon bomb damage assessments in 1991. I chose it because the grey tabby walked into my life from a Muslim household, in 1987, on a day when I happened to receive a letter claiming that fatwa author Salman Rushdie had accompanied glob-trotter Bruce Chatwin on a visit to Steep Holm to see the island's famous peonies in flower.

As for the Wincanton street-cat, he had already used up his nine lives, ten times over, when after a morning of mad misadventure in the winter of 1988 – when both of us came within inches of being squashed on the A303 – he was bought a lead. There followed a disastrous hour of distress as he clawed, bit, spat and foamed. Next morning I put the collar on again but told him this was the final attempt.

Instead, as I abandoned all hope, he strode off and walked to heel beside me, acting as if he had always been on a lead. It then took only a couple of entanglements, deep in bramble bushes, for him to learn that the secret of utilising the full four metres of his spring-loaded Flexi-cord was to follow it back and out along the course of the entry route. Having perfected the technique he would emerge at full speed without becoming entangled.

If he broke into a run somewhere harmless I would drop the lead and its plastic case. They would bounce along behind him. Inevitably, something would catch, usually around a tree-stake, and I would yell 'Stop'. He did so, instantly, as I caught up with a gentler 'Hold on'. After disentanglement he was given the all-clear, 'OK, you can go now'. Where there were direction choices, 'Left' or 'Right' normally sufficed, without recourse to a tug. 'Down the field' was always self-explanatory.

Our hunting territory came courtesy Martin Kingston and Compton Castle Estates. Their herdsman, Michael, was somewhat surprised when we turned up a mile or more from the home-range, on the other side of the valley. Martin, who cherished our wildlife, realised that this cat was a predator, though on the credit side it was Salman who took me to a sparrowhawk that was caught in the remains of an old cage, in my garden wilderness. I was able to keep one killer from another and successfully released the bird.

'Good boy' followed any action worthy of approval. 'Look' had him glancing to the right on arrival at the road. 'Trot, trot' encouraged him to run at my side.

'Keep over' had him edging against the verge as a car approached. 'Up' would get him to climb the roadside bank.

Generally it worked but dramatic lapses such as dashing straight across the road when flocks of fieldfares worked their way along the hawthorn of the main road landscaping in the frosts of February 1991. The other breach of trust when off the lead was when he suddenly bounded for a tree trunk or electricity pole with a cat's cradle of wires and conductors on top. He had no sense of safety and his weight – 15 pounds – frequently brought him to the edge of grief. Once a rotten branch snapped and he fell eight feet before claw-holding a clump of ivy midway down the trunk. Another time he reached the crows' nest in the ash but their revenge was to entice him further towards the tips of the springy branches. 'Back' and 'Down' plus some emphatic 'Jump, jump' commands brought him inwards to a controlled descent. Twice I had to meet him half way after carrying an extension ladder across two fields.

He mewed plaintively through such difficulties but this never stopped him bounding into the same trouble a week later. I usually grabbed him, or released him from the lead, on such vertical diversions, but there were a couple of times he ended up hanging from a branch. Fortunately he did not have a choke-collar, and was unharmed and unbothered, which was more than could be said for me.

A disappearance in the cottage coincided with frozen pipes early in 1991. It was the first time he had seen me open the loft-hatch. I realised he would follow up the steps, so I shut him in a bedroom. On coming down I shut the trap, removed the ladder, and opened the bedroom door.

That night he was gone. I returned from searching the great outdoors to hear a faint miaow from the ceiling. Salman came to the hatch with delight at seeing me. He kept arching his back, rubbing me, and was a purr-machine for the next hour.

Then I worked out how he had done it. The door of the middle bedroom was open to a point three feet below the loft closure. From the top of the door, Salman had launched himself at the board, with such force that it pushed up. He grappled a foothold and nudged himself through the opening. Then the hatch closed itself behind him.

The same impetuousness was shown in the garden of Fairview, next-door, where he would hurl himself over a dense conifer hedge, oblivious of what lay the other side. Much of it was Louisa Saffioti's chicken run. Country living for Salman began with rounding up her hens, just like a sheep-dog, in the Big Corn Ground (its local name) that extended for half a mile below us. He was literally caught with one in the hedge. I was surprised that a bird could have so many feathers through it looked much the same despite the losses. They soon learned to fly and became sporting game-birds. He still chased them, but refrained from chasing any of the flock, and later Salman regarded the gulls and their chicks on Steep Holm as honorary chickens.

The fox was another matter. I narrated that experience for *The Visitor* magazine in February 1991. Salman had leapt into the hedgerow at a sound which I though was my other tabby cat, Zappa, but instead a fox brushed against my leg:

'I then struggled to release the cat's lead so that he could continue chasing it to the corner of the field. From there, vital seconds having been lost in unleashing him, it was no longer hot pursuit but he insisted on bounding along the fox's trail to the stream, which is half way to Blackford. After much purring and still with a bristling tail, he turns back for home. Very brave; or very foolish.'

He never liked diminutive in-bred farm cats we encountered and would send clumps of fur blowing up the road. Smaller mammals were caught for a pastime. Even on the lead he could jump eight feet into the roadside verge from a standing start and land on a vole. That was his record – the maximum measured leap. Usually it was less impressive and the success rate about one in three. But if he caught something it was dead, usually instantly or at leat without the feline habit of playing with prey. Voles were instantly crunched and eaten with only the stomach-sack being eschewed. I never saw anything escape without my intervention, which met frenzied resistance, and I only managed to save a couple of young moles and a few shrews that probably died later from shock.

As for the voles, I tried stamping my feet to alert them, but that was counter-productive because he pounced as they moved. Twice I picked up the cat, insisted that we worked another patch, and then proceeded to put him down right on top of prey. Once it was a vole on a bank and the other time a rat on the verge. Often, when he heard something, Salman would stand up on his back feet, like an otter, to listen.

A field that had been planted with trees, of only three acres, was smothered with lank grass. Salman always visited this area, during his daily exercise hour between seven and eight o'clock in the morning. That bit of freedom was compulsory for us both – fog, rain and snow notwithstanding. It was a killing-field for all seasons. In fact the catch rate was better than average in the frost and snow.

When Salman settled at a particular spot I would hitch the lead around a suitable sapling and leave him for an hour. Then on three occasions he managed to free himself and drag the lead back home. Once it snagged in woodland and I did not find and free him until midnight. To find how he was accomplishing his Houdini act I tied the lead as usual and watched from a distance. When he was bored with lying in the grass to listen for 'vermin' he followed the lead back to its tie-band. Then with his paws and head he nudged the loop up the whip of a miniature tree and its rabbit-guard until it fell off the top. Thereafter I always fastened the lead, securely, with a short belt.

Ecologically, the population energetics of shrews in summertime and voles throughout the year can sustain high levels of predation during this transitional period of dense, deep grass, until it begins to thin as tree-cover takes over. Sometimes a kestrel worked the slope but they were more often seen in the cat-free corridor flanking the A303. Badgers and foxes occasionally crossed the triangular patch but Salman worked it much more methodically.

His daily catch-rate was usually one vole; frequently two voles; and once a week three voles. Seldom was there none. His record was six, in 40 minutes, one October morning. I calculated that he removed 500 in 1990. He was often satiated or sick. Zappa, a perpetual novice, was often the beneficiary and both cats either breakfasted outdoors or brought surplus carnage home to their food dish. Once I found a rat's head on the duvet.

Salman travelled reasonably well, silently even, provided he had not eaten in the previous eight hours. Otherwise he would moan and vomit. His favourite position was sprawled along my head-rest which was comfortable for us both. I was reprimanded for this by Maggie Lancaster on a visit to Delaware veterinary surgery in Castle Cary for his precautionary vaccinations:

'Have you carried him loose in the car? That's both dangerous and illegal.'

Zappa was also receiving medical attention and three visits later the cat family knew the ropes. Salman went up the steps first, me next, and Zappa followed behind. That time they won compliments from Miss Lancaster:

'Your cats are amazing. They are much better controlled than many of the dogs we see!'

Salman explored every room of the sprawling ground floor of Holbrook House Hotel and did his professional inspection of the four walls of each of them. No vermin there. Despite its strong spring, he even managed to push open the door to the reception office, to the surprise of manager Philip Jackson who remarked:

'That's more than some of the guests can do!'

His ideal home would have been with the Saffioti family, in East Cottage, at the cosy end of our windy ridge. Salman was obviously born into the comfort and security of a family life that is the one aspect where mine has been deficient. Hearing their door open, he ran towards it with his tail in the air, and barged his way in or – if restrained – threw himself down in a state of ecstasy on the step. Indoors, as a visitor, his behaviour was impeccable (forgetting one scratching of Olive Saffioti's carpet) but outdoors, when excited, he did like to mark his territory. Sometimes, when he was in the right mood, I could induce this with the words 'Spray, spray, spray'. Likewise I said 'Scratch, scratch, scratch' as he sharpened his claws on tree trunks or stacks of timber.

Chris Maslen, the work-horse on Steep Holm, found the spraying prospect particularly disgusting and was only a little less unhappy about the way I addressed the cat:

'You called him Salman Legg. Why did you call him Legg? He's not a person.'

Steep Holm became his adventure playground in 1989. En route to the island we frequently stopped for walkies between Marshall's Elm and Walton Hill in the Polden Hills. He spent 130 days on the island and thoroughly enjoyed every moment short of the voyage home. Arriving, he strained excitedly on the bows and was always the first to jump ashore. He then led the way up to the Barracks, via one or more diversions to investigate this and that. Cat-lover Mary Collier had told me:

'Cats should have the maximum amount of liberty that is compatible with their safety. Sometimes that's not a lot.'

Salman's freedom was doubly constrained by his capacity for misadventure and the supply of natural temptations. There being no voles on the island, he turned his attentions to the birds, but did not take on the gulls. He made an unsuccessful grab at a chiffchaff released from Tony Parsons's ringing nets – missing it by ten inches – but did account for the odd dunnock and wren. A reputation for worse was firmly established in 1990 when with growls of celebration – 'Row, row, row' he pulled along the path and then into the Barracks a freshly-killed adult rabbit. He held it by the neck and dragged it the full length of his body, between his bowed legs, along the ground. It was delivered to my bunk.

That nearly had him banned. Since then he was restricted to an hour's supervised run in the morning and a walk around the perimeter path, on the lead, at dusk. Even that did not stop him exploring. On his first day back on Steep Holm, on 30 March 1991, he was rediscovered three times. Firstly was at Monks' Wall overhanging the sheer eastern cliffs. Secondly he backed out of the barrel of Victorian cannon No. 67 at Split Rock Battery. Thirdly he emerged from beneath the Barracks floor (having earlier been seen to disappear up the rusty chimney of the kitchen stove).

Ventilation shafts were cat-proofed. Above, however, his speciality act was to climb into the exposed roof-trusses of the Barracks and then bound from beam to beam over the full length of the main hall of the building, at a height of five metres above the floor.

He was unenthusiastic about leaving – indeed words not to use near home ('Time to go in now') had their equivalent on the island ('Here comes the boat'). Salman watched intently as it neared and tried to escape back on to the island. At the other end, from half a mile out in Weston Bay, he kept his eyes on the emergent landscape and sniffed the mainland breeze.

Watch a cat's eyes! C. H. D. Grimes wrote to *The Countryman* in Autumn 1961 about being saved a long walk when a boy at Mothecombe, Devon, volunteered to go indoors and check the state of the tide at Holbeton. He returned immediately and said the tide was in. Asked how he knew, he said he could tell by the cat's eyes, and the prediction turned out to be right:

'Some years later at St Malo, on the other side of the Channel, I read in an article that before the building of the causeway that joins Mont St Michel with the mainland, Breton country people living some distance from the shore always looked at the cat's eyes to see whether the tide would allow them to cross to the Mount.'

Back home, his great black and yellow eyes out of tidal range, he was a disappointment in just one respect. My beloved earlier tabby, Piggy (1972-85) talked all the time. Salman did so on only a handful of occasions, though one was memorable. Nadia Gant, departing with husband Roland for retirement in the French Alps, looked down and said to him:

'Now, will you look after Rod?'

'Mmmn' he replied. He dutifully did so until his last illness in 1997. An x-ray then revealed that he had experienced an eventful time before coming into my life. He was truly bionic, with a pin and plastic parts holding his hips together, put there presumably after a road traffic accident. Salman always lived on the edge.

To resume my story, I see from *The Visitor* in February 1991 that I included its editor in my *Wincanton Directory*, and entered into an on-going local controversy about the future of a town centre market place by suggesting it was used for public conveniences:

'A desperately-needed urinal . . . would be the real and spiritual home of 'The Visitor' – Alice in Wonderland escapee Patrick Dunion, cardboard city look-alike and chasm-mouthed Scotch-revived corpulent ragmonger of scurrilous regurgitated tittle-tattle to the ten per cent of the masses who can read.'

The wonderful Pat Dunion was soon to leave a gap in our lives – dying of spinal cancer that he had been taking to the osteopath – and local journalism has remained lame ever since. He did for Castle Cary what Simon Regan (1942-2000) managed from Weymouth until the latter defamed John Major and fell foul of a libel action. I made a wish for 1992 that appeared in *The Visitor* and has become increasingly desired though now with the addition of e-mails, text-messaging and the rest:

'Personally and politically I wish for more time to think. One cannot unfortunately disinvent things, but it would be good to have just one day a week that was free not only of the horrors of shopping but also had no phones, no faxes, television broadcasting or radio. Many of life's problems and those of the world come about because of the opportunity and demand for instant reactions. Usually it would be better not to know about anything until six months later, and then to see it in context.'

I had a short visit to hospital that turned into one of the best days of my life. A hernia in my right groin prolapsed on an Exmoor walk and caused me to half-crawl back to the car. I had a priority appointment with the surgeon, Mr Griffith, at the Yeatman Hospital, Sherborne, and persuaded him to operate on me under local anaesthetic. Without discomfort, it was fascinating to watch, and gently done, considering it required a seven-inch cut to push the protruding parts back behind a strip of plastic gauze.

Those who experienced general anaesthetic that Friday were groggy and had lost their appetite. I, on the other hand, was hyperactive. I scoffed my tea, walked about, and wanted to take myself along the A30 to friends in Coldharbour. That was rightly vetoed due to road safety fears. I floated into the weekend on National Health Service narcotics.

My precious mobility had been restored. I proved it the following Wednesday by climbing up and down the 205 well-worn stone steps of King Alfred's Tower near Stourhead. A week after the operation I was told to visit Milborne Port Surgery to show my operation scar to a district nurse. With her back to me, opening my file, she instructed me to sit on the bed and show her the stitches. I dropped my trousers to do so. The nurse screamed as she looked up from her notes:

'What do you think you are doing? That's a hernia but you strode in here. It's as much as most of my patients can do to get through the door. And the car keys! You know you shouldn't be driving.'

Professional walking resumed but was to lose me my first full-time job for thirty years. I was head-hunted by former *Punch* publisher Peter Shaw as editor of his own glossy *Dorset* (snappily subtitled 'The Magazine For People Who Like To Explore'). It was a feet-on editorship with me being required to provide four country walks, plus rural drives and other access-related text for each issue. I managed it for three years but it was inevitable that just about every path in the county that lay on a scenic circuit would eventually appear in print.

The spat arose when I found myself on an overgrown path beside Byways Cottage at Stour Common in the Blackmore Vale. 'Fortunately, I always carry my secateurs', I told reporter Peter Dunn of the *Observer*. 'Even on the London Underground' (where I once used them to cut the toggle from my anorak as it snagged in closing doors). A couple of paragraphs from Dunn's report on 12 April 1998 explain what happened on the walk:

'Legg was trail-blazing between the village of East Stour and the wooded heights of Duncliffe Hill when he found a section of the path blocked by an overgrown farm hedge to his left and shrubs and roses from a private garden to his right. He whipped out his secateurs from the quick-draw holster strapped to his waist and then, as he said later, "all hell broke loose".

'What added piquancy to the skirmish was that the angry protagonists knew each other. The Ashbys, owners of Byways Cottage, were the design team of Dorset magazine and were astonished to see their editor leaning over the fence to prune their ragged bushes. Ashby told Legg to clear off and warned him that he would stop the walk being published. Legg protested to the magazine owner, Peter Shaw, about "editorial interference" and, when he failed to get satisfaction, resigned on the spot. He then reported the Ashbys to the Dorset County Council rights of way office.'

With the help of printer Stephen Taylor I also started my own *Dorset Country Magazine* which ran for twelve issues. It was followed by *Purbeck – the Country*

Magazine, for nine issues, followed by two as *Purbeck and Poole Magazine*. That was my happiest time with local magazines, working for Julian Davidson and Steven Pugsley at Halsgrove Media, based then in Tiverton and now at Wellington. Then, in the summer of 2002 I returned my roots, to walk again for John Newth's *Dorset Life* (which originated as my own *Dorset – the county magazine* for 114 issues). It continues my numeration and has entered 2011 with No. 383.

As for my *Times* letters, 'Colchester alternative to Albuquerque' was an excuse for Legg the polymath to deliver a lecture on Boadicea's revolt and 'Life goes on in derelict village' featured Mary Butts at South Egliston. Then, on 27 November 1999 I was shocked to read the leading letter at the top of the page, on realising that 'Press and party as arbiters of morality in politics' was mine:

'Having taken an inordinate time to recycle my newspapers, I am able to revisit a vintage front page of yours (October 10, 1998). The lead story that day had a prophetic double headline: "Hague fears outcry over peer's past: Tory plot to sink Archer's bid for mayor." The key paragraph in the report reads:
"'The revelation provides the latest sign that William Hague's team is determined to prevent the millionaire novelist's path, fearing that his colourful past may back-fire on the party."'

'Most maligned tree' on 19 January 2000, in defence of the sycamore, won the approval of a forester who grows it in exposed western Islay. 'Local dish', on 6 May, drew the attention of the Prince of Wales, as an advocate of traditional food, to 'Tasty snacks from the heart of Dorset':

'Bombay Mix in this case.'

'Ordeal by water' from 28 November 2000 won the bonus accolade of being chosen for inclusion in *Brief Letters to the Editor*:

'There is talk from time to time about substituting for England's imported national saint a native-born candidate. Now we have experienced the wettest autumn on record, consideration should be given to St Swithin, Bishop of Winchester between 852 and 862. Having a Bank Holiday on or near his day, July 15, would provide an opportunity for filling sandbags.'

'Hemingway's gloom' on 5 February 2001 concerned the two versions of the ending of *Farewell to Arms* which did not turn into 'violence-haunted language' until after the author's father blew his brains out. 'More badgers' on 13 June blamed the animals for ripping open our hedgehogs. 'Lancaster losses' on 7 March 2002 was about the bomber's first operational casualties. 'Off with her head' from 5 July made it into the next edition of collected letters. It concerned the beheading of a statue of a statue to Margaret Thatcher:

Prolific, with another couple of Purbeck titles, photographed by George Willey

Above left: *Favourite comfort food, on Studland beach*

Above centre: *Book signing at Swanage, photographed by Merle Chacksfield*

Above right: *Recovering in 2010, photographed by Graham Hiscock*

'There is a public house sign in Dorset that features a public figure with a severed head. The lady in its case is Anne Boleyn. Even without her head, Baroness Thatcher has yet to meet the criterion for usurping her, as the inn in question is the Silent Woman.'

As well as a number of letters on behalf of Open Spaces Society, I kept up my idiosyncratic appearances, with 'Friends, foes and the passage of time' on 7 January 2004. That was about the war memorial at Downside School, Somerset, which is the only one I have come across 'that records those from both sides of the conflict with alphabetical impartiality' – with Count Peter Wolff-Metternich of the Wehrmacht being followed by Lieutenant J. G. H. Moorhouse of the King's Own Scottish Borderers. 'Tree in a garden' on 6 March told how eight trees that I planted in my mother's garden in Bournemouth, in 1972, had became subject of tree preservation orders in 1998, including a spiky 'living fossil' *Pseudopanax crassifolius* from New Zealand. On 5 August I criticised the choice of 10 July 2005 to commemorate the end of the Second World War, with the comment that for many – including Anthony Eden as he chaired the Cabinet – there was bad news on 10 July 1945 (his son was missing in Burma).

One of my more obscure observations, on 7 October 2004, was that the first live outside broadcast had been from the top of Nelson's Column on 24 November 1923. Captain Peter Pendleton Eckersley transmitted 'sparrows twittering'. On a topical subject, in 'Walter under water' on 24 November, I found it appropriate for a public house serving food that the sign of the Virginia Ash, in Somerset, shows 'a servant throwing a bucket of water over a smoker' (namely Sir Walter Raleigh).

The lead-letter in *The Times* on 26 October 2006 was 'Tranquil life is not where we might expect it'. My subject was the Campaign to Protect Rural England's map of the most peaceful places in the land. These included Army ranges and their impact areas in Dorset and Wiltshire as well as military training areas from Dartmoor to Northumberland.

Ball lightning hit Maperton Ridge, Somerset, at 17.15 hours on Saturday 19 August 2006. It was an overcast afternoon, with a darkening sky as I walked up a flight of more than 50 steps from the bottom of my garden. I was accompanied by faithful cats Pussel and Sylvester. The onset of heavy spots of rain had ended their run across the stubble of a wheat field. There was no wind and the only noticeable change in the weather was that the temperature had dropped from a brief peak of 21 degrees at lunchtime to about 15 degrees for the rest of the day.

On reaching a concrete-flagged terrace beneath White Cottage, and passing a pond, I was stunned by a bright flash and a simultaneous crack of thunder. Ten feet in front of us was a dense oval of blue flame which burst from something not much bigger than a rugby ball. It rolled over the site of a bonfire and disappeared through the fence into the garden of Fairview.

The patio where this happened is at 360 feet above sea level – with a view south across to woods above Charlton Horethorne – and on the north side of the house the A303 runs along the top of the hill. Next-door, in Fairview, Julie Paniccia was sorting through a box of bric-a-brac, and looking out across her garden into the valley:

'I was frightened out of my wits. I've never seen anything like it in my life. A big red and orange flame, pointed at the front end, flashed across the window and went into the hedge behind the top chicken run.'

On the other side of the hedge, at East Cottage, Lorraine and Nick Allison and their family were indoors watching television. The electricity cut out and a car alarm was set off but there was no sign of any damage inside or out. My cats had fled in opposite directions, downwards into dense undergrowth, but returned unharmed in the following half hour. That was it. There was no other thunder or lightning either before or after the phenomena. Ball lightning is such a rarity that it was not properly described until a few years ago.

It has ghost-like qualities but can also be deadly. *The Newes* of 12 July 1665 reported the mayhem caused by a 'great grey ball' that passed through the church at Erpingham, Norfolk, during the Sunday afternoon service on 2 July that year:

'It left a great smoke and stink behind it, and in the confusion there was one man found stark dead and many others lamed, who yet continue so.'

The phenomenon must come in varying sizes as it has been described as resembling golf or tennis balls when it has materialised in mid-flight and rolled down the aisle of airliners during electrical storms. It may be relevant that the Maperton incident occurred above a terrace that was built upon land-fill rubbish including cans and scrap metal. Underground there had been a mains water leak, flowing through the recent drought, which had been repaired by Wessex Water the previous day. The leakage had run close to the surface because of the underlying geology which is Fuller's earth clay. I sensed that the energy for my fireball might have come up from the ground rather than down from the sky.

On 15 December 2006 I congratulated parishioners at Aller, Somerset, of 'celebrating their pagan roots' as they dragged boughs and branches into church for Christmas decorations. They must have regarded me as loony until, perhaps, a couple of them read this letter in that day's *Times*:

'Though the Christmas tree was a Victorian introduction, from Germany, bringing masses of vegetation indoors at midwinter goes back centuries, as diarists and Shakespeare confirm. I cannot recall biblical passages that would explain the spiritual significance of holly, ivy, mistletoe and yew. Gathering greenery seems an unlikely pursuit for the people of arid lands in and around Roman-occupied Palestine.'

I was in there again on the 28th, with 'Historic tremors' taking the paper to task for omitting three of our biggest earthquakes from a list compiled after a Christmas quake. On 7 April 2007, I remembered the Essex career of news photographer Don McPhee. We worked together on the *Basildon Standard* in the mid-1960s: I was his companion reporter:

'We battled with our sub-editor in Southend, Alf Goodale, who repeatedly rejected evocative images and demanded that pictures of events were filled with faces. One memorable shot, from an aquarium exhibition, featured a goldfish (in focus) with a young girl (out of focus) looking fascinated through the glass and water. Goodale exploded in rage: "Take it back to McPhee and tell him he's working for a local newspaper, not the [expletive] Sunday Times colour supplement. A decade later I was delighted to see virtually the same photograph, from a show in Manchester, across the back page of The Guardian. Don was appreciated at last.'

My letter on 'Biblical weather', on 11 July, recorded events recalled for Di Hooley and myself when we walked around a 'living history' exhibition organised by Edward Hoare in Stourhead village hall. An inundation of 8.75 inches of rain at Bruton, on 28 June 1917, broke the dam at the New Lake, Gasper, and washed through Bourton Foundry munitions works in Dorset. The Red Cross hospital at Plank House, Gillingham, had to be evacuated by the Army. Vivid memories came 'at one remove by now elderly sons and daughters'.

On 26 July 2007 it was own observation that was recorded. The presence of bumblebees in my untidy garden was entirely due to the attractive pink flowers of a migrant plant that conservationists try to eradicate:

'Even in the drizzle the bees queue to visit a clump of Himalayan balsam.'

Arthur Fossey in Braidwood, Lanarkshire, agreed:

'Three cheers for Rodney Legg's defence of Himalayan balsam. I would go further – at the end of summer in our garden it continues to flower long after most other plants and extends the bumble bee season by at least two weeks. Sometimes it appears to be the only food available.'

Di Hooley continues to threaten me with castration if those pink flowers and their exploding seed-pods should ever appear around her pond. On 14 August 2007, I was pontificating on Foulness artillery ranges and proposals for a new London airport. That on 5 September detailed a 'friendly-fire' incident involving rocket-firing RAF Typhoons of 266 Squadron and their virtual annihilation of the Royal Navy's 1st Minesweeping Flotilla. The Navy's own co-ordinators were to blame in calling for the attack, off Cherbourg on 27 August 1944, as I was able to confirm from the account of it to me by Commander Trevor Crick RN for *Dorset at War*.

That bumper year for *Times* letters continued on 6 October with a correction for the record on the introduction of baked beans to Britain (in 1886 when Henry John Heinz called on Fortnum & Mason's Piccadilly emporium while on holiday in England). Then on 8 October I had an anecdote about the late Ned Sherrin and our oil-paintings by Victorian artist Daniel Sherrin, about which we exchanged notes:

'No relation. He was an amiable drunk slouching around Whitstable when we

were milking cows in Langport and Bridgwater.'

The following day I heard Sherrin on the radio. The big man remained a folk hero to my generation for directing *That Was The Week That Was.* 'How was your tent last night, Ned?'

'Very comfortable, thank you. It's called Holbrook House Hotel.'

The nuttiest letter I have ever written appeared on 29 October 2008. It arose, I presume, from correspondence about food exploding in fridges. Anthony Byrde from Kimmeridge compared a German refrigerator manual with that for an Avro Lancaster. My words ('As one does') do need to be put into context:

'I have in front of me the panel of 16-lever switches from an Avro Lancaster which deals with the delivery of explosives. There are four basic settings ("Container – Distributor – Single and Salvo – Safe") but the latter comes with an opt-out: "Except for Jettison".

'That release mechanism is a copper clip that carries red lettering: "Remove only for Jettison". It would add an element of excitement to defrosting the fridge.'

If that was bonkers, then on 28 March 2009 I was able to prove that I can still be too clever by half, by wrongly implying that I'm a crossword addict:

'The crossword enthusiast E. A. C. Buckmaster, writing here on October 10, 1939, gave what he considered to be Adrian Bell's "cleverest clue" from the first 3,000 puzzles in The Times. *Clue: "It is topping to kiss a monkey (4)" Solution: "Apex".'*

The weather – 'Hottest in the south' – provided the letter on 14 July 2009. Though the 1976 summer is credited with the longest heatwave, the hottest day was at Brogdale, near Faversham, at 38.5C (101.3F) on 10 August 2003. The warmest July day, at Wisley, was 37.5C (99F) on 19 July 2006, to beat a long-standing record from Epsom, set in 1911:

'For the best chance of an exceptional summer it helps to live in Surrey or Kent.'

Harry Patch, the last fighting soldier of the Great War, died in 2009. My brief encounter with him that provided a 'Lives remembered' paragraph for *The Times* on 29 July:

'When in his 110th year Harry Patch signed for me a contemporary account of the third Battle of Ypres at Passchendaele. He added his Army number (29295) and "C Company, 7th D.C.L.I." for the 7th Battalion, Duke of Cornwall's Light Infantry. What amazed a military man half his age was that

137

he was doing this and commenting on a sentence from the book without using glasses. "Harry, I can't read that," the officer said. "That's because you wear those things," he replied.'

That footnote to history was followed at the top of the same column, on 10 October 2009, with more detailed but distant memories though John Newth, the editor of *Dorset Life*, felt I should have kept the information to myself:

'My first brush with Helen Brotherton came in 1972 when, with Kenneth Allsop, I tried through my Dorset magazine to prevent Powerstock Common becoming a Forestry Commission plantation. "Too wild to be of any interest," she said, which was discreetly forgotten as joint efforts led to Dorset Wildlife Trust turning it into its flagship nature reserve.

'Her greatest victory lay in convincing British Gas and BP that the £570 million project to bring the Purbeck oilfield on-line had to be a civil engineering exemplar for civil engineering in a fragile ecosystem. Visiting her in Poole, to persuade her to be pragmatic on this and other issues, our chats touched on homosexual law reform. Her golden retriever was called Sapho.'

My next letter in *The Times* was on 'the great eccentric of Victorian Dorset', John Wanley Sawbridge-Ernle-Erle-Drax as 'The Silent MP' (11 December 2009). His successor, Richard Drax, 'will not have to work hard to emulate the parliamentary achievements'. In death, until it was demolished, Drax of the many names arranged for *The Times* 'to be delivered every day through the letter-box in his Byzantine-style mausoleum beside Holnest church in the Blackmore Vale'. Like Sawbridge Drax, I share Sir Henry 'Chips' Channon's diary entry for 4 June 1951:

'How riveting newspapers can be. It is terrible to contemplate that one day one will be dead, and never again be able to read **The Times.***'*

My next letter was about the opening performance in Abbey Road Studios (20 February 2010). This was Sir Edward Elgar's *Falstaff*, recorded on Armistice Day in 1931, and not *Land of Hope and Glory* as widely reported. The next letter was inspired by John Clare's mention of a crane, in a poem, which might have been misidentification for a heron. My contrary evidence documented (21 August 2010) how up to eight cranes at a time were being seen on the Essex marshes in the 1880s. At least one, shot and stuffed, went to Saffron Walden Museum.

The next letter 'Beamed in' on 13 September to explain code-names for the wartime German 'Knickebein' (Crooked Leg or Dog Leg and a cocktail) signal for blind-bombing and British counter-measures 'Headaches' and 'Aspirins'. In 'Brutal memorial' on 29 September I defended the design of the Bomber Command statuary in Green Park with the comment that 'the real shame is that it was not erected decades ago'. That was something of a milestone as my 65th contribution to *The Times*. It was followed on 30 December by a letter on the Great Escape from Stalag Luft III in 1943. Then came a comment on George VI's stammer.

The year 2010 changed my life. My last proper drink was to celebrate John Pitfield's 50th birthday at the Brace of Pheasants, Plush, at 8 pm on 23 February. I was home early that evening with chronic stomach pain and was admitted for tests to Yeovil District Hospital on 10 March. Having confidently walked in - lugging a case with 600-page books for light reading – I was suddenly confined to a wheelchair and told my heartbeat was haywire. The figures alternated between 20 and 230 beats a minute. I refused to have my heart stopped and re-started, on being told there was a one-in-200 chance of triggering a brain haemorrhage, and reassured that this was 'no real risk'. I disagreed:

'Those are sniper's odds. Either for taking a shot at someone or risking being shot yourself. I'm not going to war on another front – this isn't the time for invading Poland.'

I was pathologically note-taking through intensive care and the rest of my month inside. I persevered with shaving at day-break and forced myself to hobble along the corridor, dragging leads and tubes, as many times as possible. Then I looked forward to Di Hooley's loyal evening appearances – more something out of *Vogue* than Florence Nightingale – to tuck me into bed. It was a real art and skill to arrange pillows under my feet and sides to alleviate gross swelling of toes, legs and scrotum. Surplus fluid also blocked my phone-ear.

The heart problem turned out to be atrial fibrillation from the right aorta. Like an estimated 700,000 Britons, I have gone through my life without realising the condition, which is controlled by beta-blockers. Their effect, in the month that the drug's discoverer died, was dramatic. As I read the obituary of 85-year-old analytical pharmacologist and Nobel laureate Sir James Black, Order of Merit, my heart rate stabilised at 77 and went into normal sinus rhythm. The second difficulty to be sorted out was an intestinal blockage, initially caused by peanuts at Christmas, which required an operation. The third diagnosis was pancreatic cancer, from which dour Scot consultant Mr J. Ockrim and fellow oncologist Dr Gotto said I probably had only two or three months to live, with palliative chemotherapy being all they could offer. Dr Geoff Sparrow estimated a 30 per cent chance of it causing the cancer to shrink or slow.

Once released, over Easter, I soon attempted resuming normal walkies. Slowly I managed to reach two kilometres a day (stretched to two miles if the ground is flat) but have trouble negotiating decrepit gates and stiles. Previously I used to vault over barbed-wire fences. Hills now make me breathless and the effect of disability is that what used to take an afternoon can spread over a week. Walks for publication are compiled by instalments.

On the other hand I enjoy expeditions more than ever. The last few months have been a bonus. You appreciate the gift of life so much better when you are aware of its fragility.

*On the county boundary at
Stalbridge, photographed by
Stewart Canham*

Index of People and Places

INDEX